# Touched By An ANGEL

## A Christmas Miracle

### MARTHA WILLIAMSON

### EXECUTIVE PRODUCER

Novelization by Sharon Y. Cobb
based on the episodes:
"Fear Not!"
Written by Ken LaZebnik
"The Feather"
Teleplay by Valerie Woods & Ken LaZebnik
Story by Valerie Woods & Ken LaZebnik
& Robin Sheets
based on the television series created by John Masius

THOMAS NELSON PUBLISHERS
Nashville • Atlanta • London • Vancouver

Published in Nashville, Tennessee, by Thomas Nelson, Inc., and distributed in Canada by Word Communications, Ltd., Richmond, British Columbia, and in the United Kingdom by Word (UK), Ltd., Milton Keynes, England.

Scripture quotations are from the NEW KING JAMES VERSION of the Bible. Copyright © 1979, 1980, 1982, Thomas Nelson, Inc., Publishers

ISBN 0-7852-7129-5

Printed in the United States of America

2 3 4 5 6 7 — 03 02 01 00 99 98 97

Photos on pages 47 and 49 by Gregory Cannon / CBS.

# DEDICATION

This book is dedicated to Randy and Elizabeth Travis for their love, their support, their music, and their belief in "the little show that could." Dear friends, good people. Thank you.

# FOREWORD

The secretaries and assistants and coordinators have been hovering around my office door all afternoon, awaiting the last page of *A Christmas Miracle*. Actually, it's the first page of this book—the foreword. It seemed only right to welcome you to this volume with a story of the actual miracles behind the making of "Touched by an Angel's" beloved holiday episodes. There are so many anecdotes—how country music legend Randy Travis miraculously recovered from back surgery a week before we began shooting. Or the tale of the network executives who asked us to "take the Christmas out of the Christmas episode" the day before the cameras rolled. Or the story of the Salt Lake City extras who shed real tears during the filming of the stunning finale. These are the stories I usually love to share about our show. But for some reason, today I lacked the inspiration to tell them again.

I mentioned this to one of the hovering assistants as I went to lunch. I returned to my office an hour later to discover that the staff had decorated my entire office with Christmas decorations—snowmen, wreaths, Santas, and of course, angels. What with this being August, it was a funny and touching effort to inspire me. Probably desperate, too. Because they know I rarely have a problem thinking of something to write.

Only once before did I struggle to find inspiration. Coincidentally, it was when we needed an idea for what would be our first and possibly last Christmas episode. It was a hot October day in 1994. The ratings for our new little show were terrible, the reviews were worse, and the predictions were that CBS would cancel us before we even finished filming the Christmas show. Everyone said it was a hopeless cause. I suppose that's what made me want to make the Christmas show even more special than just another heartwarming holiday tale. I wanted something that reminded people of what Christmas was really about. I didn't want to warm their hearts, I wanted to jump-start them. I didn't want anyone to come to the end of the show and do anything less than rejoice. The question was . . . how? I had no ideas. None. No inspiration whatsoever.

Then Ken LaZebnik had a germ of a thought. Ken is a sensitive, charming writer for television as well as radio's Prairie Home Companion. He has a wonderful sense of the beauty to be found in simplicity, in the plain and the straightforward. And this idea of his was typically simple and yet profound. It was a vision, actually. He saw a tiny church Christmas pageant, the standard manger-and-cardboard-donkey nativity on the altar. And high above, an angel. Our angel, Monica.

That was all it was. A real angel hovering over a make-believe stable.

It was a start, but I lacked the inspiration to give it life. Then I remembered something Della Reese had said on set once: "Information comes from people, *inspiration* comes from God." She gave me a wonderful example. "You got a problem and you think you can't do something. Then you see a flower and a bee lands on it and suddenly you remember that according to the law of physics, bees can't fly. Now, that's information you KNOW. But the *inspiration* that God gives you is: maybe you can do the impossible, too. Inspiration is God revealing the truth in the information you've got."

So, I took Della's advice. I asked God for "inspiration in the information." Okay Lord, I've got a stable and an angel. Now what?

I put Handel's "Hallelujah Chorus" on the stereo and waited for an answer. (God knew I was on a deadline). I listened to the "Hallelujah Chorus" all the way through. I turned up the volume and listened to it again, and then again, and again, ten times at least. I paced back and forth through my living room. I sang along. Then I began to cry. Words on paper can never convey the soaring, spirit-lifting, soul-squeezing joy in that incomparable anthem to the glory of God. The voices proclaimed, "And He shall reign forever and ever!" and I knew that God had just showed me the truth: What were angels doing there? Bringing the good news and praising God, singing "Glory to God in the Highest and on Earth, Peace and Goodwill to Men." Hallelujah! That was the message. It's always been the message. And it would be our Christmas show.

I learned a simple lesson that day and today I was reminded of it again: God uses everything and anything to inspire us, bees and music and desperate co-workers and Della Reese and all His other wonderful creations. We just have to ask Him. I hope that this Christmas tale serves as the "information" and that God in His love will bless you with His inspiration and bring you great joy this Christmas and always.

Martha Williamson
Los Angeles, 1997

# CHAPTER
## *One*

## A Christmas Miracle

**A** pickup truck stopped in front of the Washington Park Community Church and a young man jumped out. Joey was seventeen and his high-water pants and old-fashioned wool parka gave a first impression that things weren't quite right with the teenager. In truth, Joey was sweet, compassionate, and slow. A degree of mental retardation made him an easy target for ridicule by the local kids. That was one of the reasons his big brother Wayne drove him to the church's Christmas pageant rehearsal.

After the tragic death of his parents five years earlier, Wayne felt obligated to take care of Joey, and that day the responsibility was weighing heavily upon his shoulders.

Joey hurried up the sidewalk toward the church. He stopped in his tracks, tapped himself on the head like he was trying to get his brain to wake up, then ran back to the truck where Wayne held out a paper bag through the open

# A Christmas Miracle

passenger window. Joey took the bag. "Thanks, Wayne. I forgot that."

The frustration of having to remind Joey about every little thing was clear on Wayne's face. "Think, Joey."

But Joey was oblivious to the realities of their situation, and like a child he always wanted his big brother to have more fun with him. "Why don't you come, too?"

"I gotta work, Joey. You know that."

"But…"

"Joey, no. I'll see you at five."

A worried look shadowed Joey's face as he became more animated. "Come back before five! It gets dark at five!"

Wayne put the truck in gear and tried to control his impatience with his little brother. "You gotta stop this!" As Joey watched, the old green truck drove away.

Used to this disappointment, Joey stood alone for a long moment until a gentle voice came from behind him. "Come on, Joey, we're gonna be late." Joey turned to see his best friend Serena, with her teddy bear, Mr. Beans. He took her hand, and the two friends walked into the church together as angels, Monica and Tess watched their next assignments from the balcony above.

"He's afraid of the dark?" Monica asked Tess.

"The only light that boy has in his life is his friend," Tess nodded, indicating Serena. "But light is a powerful thing, Monica. And the light from that little girl must reach into the darkest corners of Joey's life. It's gotta strengthen that boy's faith, it's gotta illuminate his brother's soul and it must burn brighter than it ever has before," she sighed, "…before it goes out." Monica looked at her with concern.

# CHAPTER
*Two*

*J*oey had to concentrate hard. Pinning a pair of fabric-and-wire wings and a tinsel halo on eight year old Serena wasn't easy for him, but he was determined as she stood on a pew near the front of the little church.

On the stage, a choir of fifteen well-meaning parishioners struggled to get through the hard parts of Handel's "Hallelujah Chorus." "Hallelujah! Hallelujah!" They sang off-key, missed the timing of every syllable, and didn't seem to have any hope of improving before the big night. Edna, in her own domineering style, played the ailing pipe organ, trying to keep everyone together.

Some of the vocalists were on stage serving as nativity players. There were also three wise men who rehearsed in street clothes, carrying brooms and shoe boxes as staffs and gifts. A bare plywood-and-cardboard mess that was barely propped up passed for a stable, but it still lacked the basic

# A Christmas Miracle

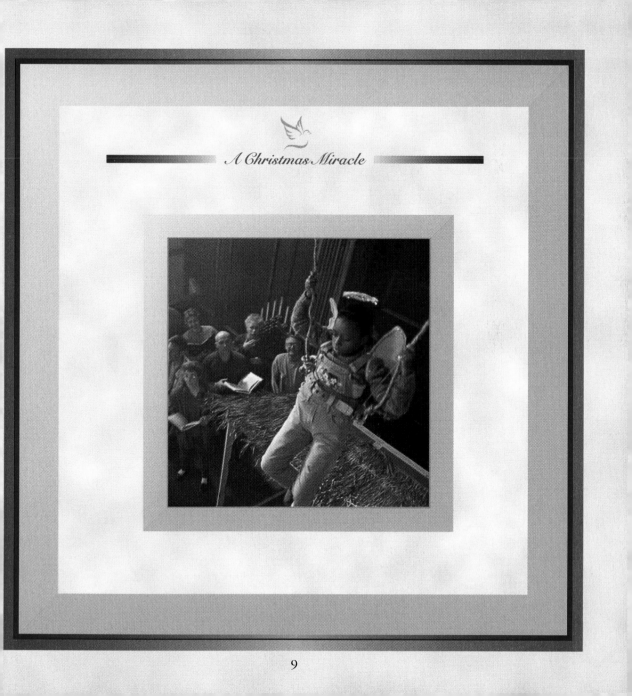

elements of a manger and hay. Serena's mother sat and watched from a front-row pew.

A screeching, wheezing noise came from the organ, then it sounded its last note. Edna kept her cool, but groans from the choir betrayed their impatience. "Oh, no." "Here we go again."

Edna rose up from the antique bench that held her generous girth and took a look at the towering brass pipes behind the keyboard. "I told you this organ would die before I did."

Joey finished his angel-wing duty and turned to see the choir in disarray as everyone encircled the organ. "Oh, no." He helped Serena down off the pew and headed to the front.

Beside the stage, Harry, a strong man with a determined look on his face, was not aware of the mini-catastrophe below and feverishly worked on a pulley system. He called over to Edna, "Keep going. I'll get it working!"

Edna looked over at him. "I can't keep going, fool! We're not waiting for you, we're waiting for this old piece of…"

"Excuse me." Tess and Monica arrived as if on cue carrying tool boxes. "We're from Seraphim Organ Service." Everyone turned to see them as they came up the aisle.

"We didn't call any service. You'd better check with the pastor. Deacon Jamison, did Pastor Mike mention anything to you about organ service?"

Deacon Jamison, a polite man in a polka-dot bow tie with a sweater and big glasses, shook his head.

Tess spoke up. "Oh, this is covered under a service agreement."

"But this organ's a hundred years old."

"It was a lifetime guarantee."

"Well, you're too late." Edna looked at the organ, a lost cause.

Monica appealed directly to Deacon Jamison with her most charming smile. "Oh, you never know. It's going to be a beautiful Christmas pageant." The good deacon nodded agreeably.

"Except now there's no music." Joey was worried—concerned that if there was no music, there wouldn't be a Christmas show. And if there was no Christmas pageant, his best friend Serena wouldn't get to be an angel.

Tess reassured Joey, "You leave that to us."

What did they have to lose? If the organ was under a lifetime warranty and the two strangers could fix it, the pageant would have a chance. Edna's face lit up. She went into action doing what Edna did best—taking charge. "Okay, folks. Shepherds, back to your field. Wise men, places."

"You know, the shepherds were over there." Tess pointed to the other side of the stage, remembering the original manger scene in intimate detail.

For a moment, it looked like Edna didn't appreciate Tess butting into her business, her Christmas pageant. She looked over at the shepherds. "Back by the altar."

Tess couldn't help herself. "They were west of the manger. And Balthasar was in front."

One of the wise men, Balthasar, raised his hand to his deaf ear. "What?"

"It was Balthasar and then Melchoir and then Caspar, and the shepherds were cowering right about there…"

Edna gave Tess a vinegary look. "Is this from your imagination…or from memory?" Proud of what she thought was an exceptionally clever remark, she dared Tess to reply.

Tess didn't back down. She flashed a genuine smile at Edna, raised an eyebrow, and said, "Honey, you'd be surprised what I remember."

The two women squared off. Edna, whose mother and grandmother before her had led the choir at the church, stepped forward to the edge of the stage and looked down at Tess. "Well, sister, if you know the score so well, why don't you just lead the band?"

Tess leaped at the invitation. "Well, if you insist." She put her tool box down and took the reins. "Shepherds, over there, and get closer together."

Bewildered, Edna couldn't believe that the choir was actually following the stranger's directions so responsively. She was peeved and took a seat in a pew on the first row waiting for Tess to make a fool of herself.

Serena saw her chance to get Joey involved in the pageant. "Joey, go over and be a shepherd."

Joey was reluctant, but with Serena's warm encouragement he ran over to the shepherds and took his place. Serena was having trouble adjusting her halo when Monica stepped in. "Let me help you. These things can be tricky."

"Thanks."

"You're going to be a beautiful angel, Serena."

"I can't wait." Serena beamed and went to her mother in the front row. "Mommy, you have to go home now."

Serena's mom took her hand, admiring her angelic wardrobe. "Why, sweetheart?"

"It's a surprise. You can't see until it's real."

"Well…"

"Please, Mommy!"

Serena's mother gave in to her little girl's tenacity. "Okay. When should I come get you?"

From the stage a few feet away, Joey had been listening and shouted a little too loudly, "Can Serena come to my house?"

Serena looked up at Joey admiringly, then back at her mom. "Yeah, I'll go home with Joey."

Joey clapped his hands excitedly. "Yeah! We can make macaroni again! She makes good macaroni. I'll take care of her!"

Serena's mother got up, glad that her little girl had such a good friend in Joey. "I know you will, Joey. You say hi to Wayne for me." She hugged her daughter. "I'll pick you up tonight at Joey's."

When her mother was gone, Serena took off for the stage.

Tess got the rehearsal started. "Places, please."

From the front-row pew, Edna challenged Tess again. "You sure you've done this before?"

Confidence broke out on Tess's face in the form of a big smile and she said to Edna, "It's gonna be just like being there." Then she turned to the choir. "Notes, please. We're gonna run this a cappella until we get that organ in shape."

Edna stood up. "It better be in shape by Sunday night." She gave Tess a look as disparaging as she dared while under the roof of the church, blew a note on the pitch pipe, raised her hands to direct the choir, and bellowed off-key, "Hallelujah!"

Tess stopped her. "You can sit down." Edna frowned and gave Tess an even more belittling look than the first as the choir took its notes and hummed, directed by Tess.

Looking apprehensive, Joey approached Edna and whispered, "This is going to be at night?"

Edna nodded. "Sunday night, seven o'clock. Maybe you can get your brother to come." Joey's eyes dropped with the realization that the pageant would take place at night. He turned and walked away. Then Edna sat down on the pew, crossing her arms, and listened to a woeful rendition of the Hallelujah Chorus.

Tess stopped the cacophony of clashing vocals, put her hand to her head, and took a deep breath. "Choir, a little feeling, please. Shepherds, think awe! A heavenly host has just appeared before your eyes. Think wonder! Think awe!"

The shepherds gave her their best awestruck poses. No Oscar contenders here, but Tess was encouraged. "That's good. That's good. Okay...action!"

Deacon Jamison bound onto center stage in front of the stable. "And lo, there were in the same country shepherds keeping watch over their flocks by night. And behold, an angel of the Lord stood by them, and the brightness of God showed round about them, and they were greatly afraid, and the angel said to them..."

As he spoke, Serena in her angel wings and halo, rose in a harness attached to a pulley from the back of the stable.

At the side of the stage, Harry cranked the frayed rope as their little angel ascended over the wise men and cast of players. But something was wrong. Serena was out of breath. She tried her best to deliver her lines. "Fear not! I bring you good tidings of great joy that will be to all men…" Halfway across the sanctuary, the pulley jammed. Harry struggled to free the line, but nothing happened. Serena gasped for breath as she hung there helpless in midair. The choir stopped singing. A hush came over the assembly.

Joey realized that Serena was in trouble. "Serena! Serena!" He raised his arms up to her. "Serena! I'll catch you! Don't fall! I'll catch you!"

The room was in chaos, everyone talking at once, circling the little girl dangling from the harness. Harry worked the crank, but it wouldn't move. He shouted, "She's not gonna fall!" But Joey didn't hear him, and was becoming more frantic by the moment. "I'll catch you, Serena!" Edna tried to quiet him.

"Calm down, Joey."

Harry fumbled with the hand-crank. "This dad-blamed thing!" From the sanctuary, Monica saw Harry almost panicking and Serena gasping for air. She stepped forward, focusing on the jammed pulley, and suddenly the rope began to move, lowering Serena down. Harry watched incredulously as the rope moved through the crank, even though the crank arm remained jammed and motionless.

Gasping for breath, Serena descended into the safety of Joey's waiting arms. The others gathered around. One of the shepherds helped as Serena touched the stage floor. "Here you go, honey."

Deacon Jamison supervised the successful rescue. "Piece of cake. Good job, Harry!"

Harry was confounded. The pulley was still frozen, immovable. He knew he had nothing to do with it all.

"I can't breathe." Serena collapsed in Joey's arms. He was in a panic over his best friend's condition. Deacon

Jamison knelt on the floor beside them. "Let's give her some air."

Joey's eyes were wide and serious. "I was scared, Serena. I was scared." The deacon patted Serena empathetically. "You're going to be okay. Want me to call your folks?" She shook her head bravely. "I'm okay." But she wasn't.

She started to cough. Monica made her way to the circle and put a gentle hand on Serena. Suddenly, the coughing stopped and Serena got her breath back a bit. The little girl's only concern was whether she would get to be an angel in the pageant, and she looked over at Harry, who was examining the flying harness, and pleaded, "It's going to work, isn't it?"

"I'm not gonna let you down, honey."

"I gotta fly."

"She has to be the angel." Joey made sure everyone knew.

Edna leaned over Serena. "You'll fly, honey. You're the only angel we got."

*A Christmas Miracle*

Tess and Monica exchanged a sad, insightful look. It was days like that when being God's messengers was most difficult, and when knowing what angels know accommodated a special understanding of the fine line between heaven and earth.

# CHAPTER *Three*

Life is a series of tests. Tests of compassion, tests of faith, tests of fear. When you're young like Joey and Serena those tests can seem insurmountable, yet that's when the strongest shines the brightest.

The two buddies sat on the church steps waiting for Joey's big brother to pick them up. Joey searched the late afternoon sky for any sign of darkness. "That rope scared me." His breath was visible in the cold air as he spoke.

"I know, Joey. But don't worry, I'll be okay."

"I don't think you should go on that rope. It's too scary."

"I've got to, Joey. This is my only chance to be an angel."

"You could do it next year."

She searched for a way to explain the unexplainable. Then she said, "I'll be too big by then. The church doesn't have any little kids my size. I gotta do it now."

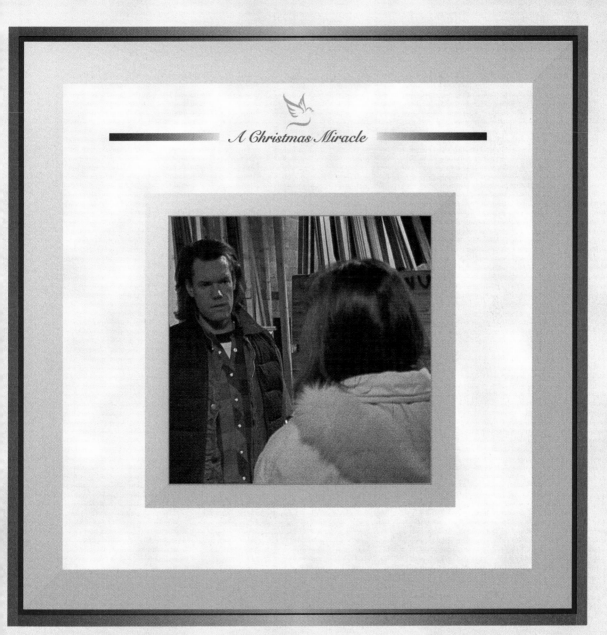

*A Christmas Miracle*

The front door opened and Edna came out, followed by Tess. Monica was with them, Serena's bear, Mr. Beans, in her arms.

Still annoyed with Tess commandeering her choir, Edna, shaking her head barked, "Well, what do you mean, the pipes are dirty?"

"I mean they're dirty. There's been a lot of hot air blown through those things."

Edna snorted, turned up the collar on her coat, and headed down the sidewalk into the chilly breeze.

As Monica passed Serena and Joey on the steps, she handed the little girl her teddy bear. "Serena, look what you forgot!" Serena hugged the well-worn green bear to her chest. "Mr. Beans!"

"Is somebody coming to take you two home?"

Joey looked up at her anxiously. "Yeah. Before it gets dark. I have to be home before dark. It's not getting dark, is it?"

"No, not yet."

Knowing Joey can be forgetful sometimes, Serena asked, "Wayne's coming to pick you up, right?"

An empty look came over Joey's face. "I think. I said I'd see him before dark." He rapped on his head with his knuckles, like he was trying to jar something loose inside. Why did this always happen to him? Everything seemed so clear a moment ago, now it's all a blank. "I can't remember. What if it gets dark and he doesn't come? I have to be home before it gets dark."

Serena took up for her pal protectively. "He's not afraid of the dark. He just doesn't like it very much."

Monica nodded sympathetically. "Maybe I could give you a ride home, Joey. And Tess will wait here, just in case your brother comes."

Tess pointed to the curb where a long, red Cadillac convertible was parked. "See that big red boat over there? That's my car. Not many people get to ride in that."

"Wow!" Joey was impressed. Besides, that meant that he would get home before sunset. He jumped up and ran toward the car, but hearing Serena cough, he stopped and helped her through the snow.

As Monica watched, she sighed. "It's hard sometimes, Tess. Knowing the what and not always knowing the why. Knowing more than human beings and less than God."

"When life keeps you in the dark, that's when you start looking for stars."

The gray sky darkened with the coming of a cold winter night as the Cadillac pulled up in front of a little house blanketed by pure white snow. Joey hopped out, followed by Serena, and they headed into the house with Monica.

Joey bolted through the front door into the living room, calling for his brother. "Wayne! Wayne! I'm home! Don't pick me up!" Joey's face was alight as he looked for Wayne. "I just beat the dark."

Wayne, coat in hand, didn't look glad to see Joey. "What are you doing here? I was on my way to get you. What if I'd missed you?" It wasn't that Wayne didn't love Joey, and it wasn't that he was angry that Monica had brought his little brother home. It was just that this was one more thing that didn't happen as planned. One more thing that didn't go right. Life with Joey was like that. And Wayne was running out of patience. "Why don't you listen to me?"

"Monica gave me a ride, Wayne."

Monica came in the door and waved hello to Wayne. Realizing he should be grateful, he let his aggravation at Joey go and thanked Monica. He invited her in, and greeted Serena as she and Joey headed into the kitchen to make macaroni and cheese. Joey stopped a moment, introduced Monica to Wayne, then turned to his brother. "Wayne, the stable fell over. Can you fix it?" So here was another thing. It was always something with Joey. "Wayne! Can you fix it? Can you fix the stable? You have lots of wood and hammers and stuff."

"Yeah. Well…"

Joey quickly disappeared into the kitchen with Serena. Wayne explained to Monica, "I've got a lumber yard in town. What are you doing around here?"

"I'm working on the organ at the church."

"I haven't been inside there for years. Is that old thing still pumping?"

"Just barely. But we'll get it fixed in time for the pageant. Are you going?"

Wayne shook his head. "I'm not a Christmas kind of guy."

"Everybody loves Christmas."

"We keep it pretty low-key around here," said Wayne.

"What do you mean?"

He looked through the kitchen door and saw Joey and Serena busy at the counter. "We don't make a big deal out of it. When our folks were alive, our mom went all out every year, but I'm too busy for that stuff now."

"What about St. Patrick's Day? Or the Fourth of July? Do you celebrate those?"

"You know what I celebrate? I..." He checked the kitchen again to make sure the kids weren't within earshot, then quietly admitted, "I celebrate every day that goes by that Joey hasn't broken something or spilled something or ripped something or hugged somebody too hard or screamed his lungs out if it got dark when he wasn't looking. That's what I celebrate. And when it happens, it usually doesn't last very long."

"Being a caregiver isn't easy."

"Thank God for Serena. She takes him off my hands for a while. Doesn't let anybody tease him or hurt him. Probably the only one who can really handle him." They glanced at the two friends happily cooking together in the kitchen, then he conceded, "Maybe that's something to celebrate."

A moment went by, then Monica became solemn. "Wayne, I learned something about Serena today that maybe you should know."

"It's about her heart, right? I heard she has some kind of defect."

"It's a viral disease." Monica studied his eyes. "It's incurable."

Wayne didn't know what to say. Incurable. That had to be wrong. "I thought it was one of those childhood things you grow out of."

Monica shook her head. "Some children survive longer than others, but in Serena's case..." She looked at little Serena in the next room who was carefully pouring milk into a bowl as Joey watched. "Wayne, Joey is going to lose his best friend very soon."

Wayne looked away, the words ringing in his ears. How would Joey survive losing his only friend, one of the only people who made his little brother feel normal? And who would help him take care of Joey when Serena was gone?

Laughter lilted from the kitchen as Joey and Serena made macaroni and cheese, along with childhood memories. Memories that Joey would cherish for a very long time.

# CHAPTER *Four*

*A*ngels cannot change the past, nor can they predict or see into the future. But they are given revelations from God, which they are obligated to reveal to humans. So it was in Serena's case. And when the right time came, Tess and Monica would be there for the little girl.

The tinseled edges of Serena's fabric-and-wire wings sparkled in the late afternoon light from the stained glass window. Monica helped her get them into place, commenting about Serena's green bear, "I have it on very good authority that angels don't normally carry dolls."

Immediately Serena corrected her—it wasn't a doll, it was Mr. Beans. Monica suggested that Mr. Beans might qualify as a cherub, a baby angel. Serena looked at her teddy, coughed, and said, "Mr. Beans isn't a baby. He's older than I am. He's

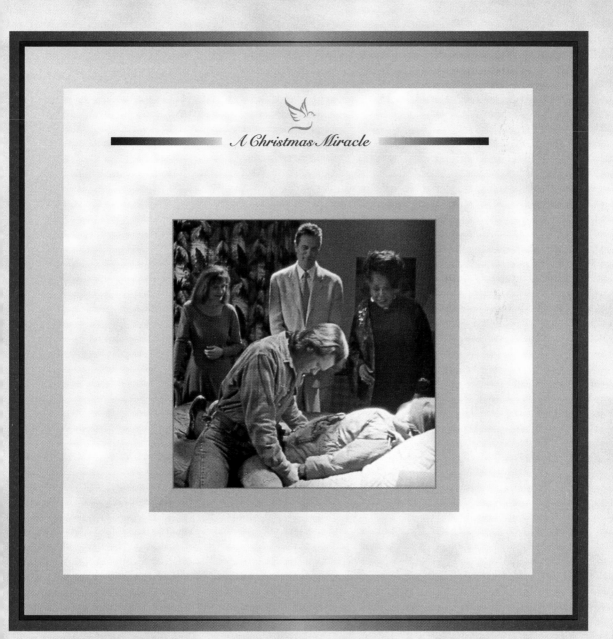

*A Christmas Miracle*

got to fly with me. I promised him. An angel keeps her promises, doesn't she?" Monica confirmed that, indeed, angels always kept their promises.

Near the stage, beside the pulley for the angel harness, Deacon Jamison and Harry inspected the contraption. They talked about how it looked dangerous, but that Serena had her heart set on it. And since they couldn't give her a new heart, the least they could do was give her this.

Joey quietly painted a cardboard sheep for the nativity scene. It took all the concentration he had to get the brush strokes almost even. Serena and Monica had been watching for a minute or two before he realized that they were there. He looked up, then proudly back at his work, which they said was beautiful. In the background Tess and Edna rehearsed the choir in the Hallelujah Chorus. It was truly awful. Even Tess couldn't get a harmonious chord out of the calamity. When they hit a particularly out of tune bar, both Serena and Joey winced at the sound. Serena tried not to laugh. "That really sounds terrible."

"They're rehearsing. In the end, it will sound…" Monica cringed at another off-key note, then continued, "…better."

"Can't they sing 'Silent Night?' That's my favorite." Joey agreed that it was his favorite too, and Monica assured them that they would get to sing "Silent Night" at the pageant.

Joey stopped painting and looked up at them with sad eyes. "I'm not coming to the pageant."

Monica was surprised. "What? Joey, you must come. You've done so much to make it happen."

He looked embarrassed and anxious. "Well, I'm not going. Don't you know when it is? Nobody said when it is." Serena explained quietly to Monica that Joey didn't ever go out at night, but reassured Joey that they'd figure out something.

Joey glanced nervously at the darkening window. "Why isn't Wayne here? It's getting dark. I can't go outside when it's dark."

"What is it about the dark that frightens you, Joey?" Monica wanted to know.

"People who go out in the dark don't come back."

Outside, a horn blew. It sounded like Wayne's truck horn, but Joey refused to go out. The sun was setting and the blackness of night was coming too fast. Wayne came through the door to get Joey, who became more and more agitated and let Wayne know that he was late—too late. Wayne's patience with Joey ended there.

He took Joey by the arm. "I don't have time for this tonight. Come on. We'll hop in the truck and be home before you know it." But Joey pulled away. It became a battle of wills: Wayne's powerful insistence that they go, Joey's frantic refusal to venture into the darkness.

Finally Serena stepped in, calming Joey with her understanding. She showed him how to put his hand over his eyes so that he could not see the dreaded twilight.

"It's not really dark. It's kind of like 'Silent Night,' okay? All is calm, all is bright. All is bright, get it?"

She led him out the door to Wayne's truck.

When they got home, Joey knew that Wayne was not happy about what had happened at the church. He also knew that

Wayne had been late because he had to get a special order out down at the lumber yard and now he had to go back to work. So when Wayne took his coat off in the living room, Joey thought he had changed his mind and would stay there with him. Joey was glad about this until Wayne said, "Joey, sit down. We gotta talk."

Joey had heard those words before. He never wanted to hear them ever again. Those words led to trouble. The world went upside down the last time Wayne had said those words, so Joey tried to change the subject. But Wayne insisted that he sit down and listen to what he had to tell him.

"The last time you said that, it was…it was about Mom and Dad." Joey hurried around the coffee table and headed for the stairs. "They went out in the dark and didn't come back and then you said, 'Sit down, I need to talk to you.'"

Wayne stopped him and tried to start talking again, but Joey wrapped his arms around his head, covered his ears, and screamed, "No, no, no, no, no!"

So, Wayne gave up on telling Joey about Serena. It was hard enough without Joey making it any more difficult. It'd have to wait until a better time.

The next day, after practice, Joey and Serena descended from the church into the freshly fallen snow. Tess and Monica watched as they went. It had been a good rehearsal. Things were coming together—slowly. Monica almost had the organ working and Tess had become indispensable to the choir. But their real job there was just beginning.

Serena looked back at "the organ ladies" at the door and waved as she and Joey headed down the street. Joey peered over at the horizon. The sun was two fingers from the top of the trees. Plenty of time to get home safely.

The two friends trudged through the snow together. Joey noticed that Serena was still wearing her halo. She said she liked it and was wearing it as her hat. They came upon an especially inviting bank of powdery snow where Serena tossed

Mr. Beans onto the ground, plopped down, and spread her arms out to make a snow angel. Joey was nervous about getting home, but couldn't resist the fun.

So there they were, lying in the snow, talking like they always did. And Joey said, "I'm sorry about yesterday, Serena. I made myself embarrassed."

She reassured him that everyone was afraid of something. Then he asked, "What do you do when you're scared?"

"Sometimes I talk to God."

"What do you say?"

She looked over at him and said earnestly, "I close my eyes and try to get very quiet and then let Him listen to my heart. But that's just me. I like the way you pray, Joey. I hear you in church." Then she recommended that he talk to God about being afraid of the dark. Joey thought this was a good idea and added that he could also ask God to make Wayne like him better, too.

Suddenly Serena began to cough and gasp for breath. He knew something was terribly wrong. He looked up and down the street, but didn't see anyone. Joey wanted to give in to panic, but he knew he was the only one who could help her. He couldn't let her down.

Joey knelt beside her, got his arms around her little body, and lifted her up. "Serena, I'll get you home. Hold on."

He carried her as best he could toward home, leaving Serena's halo and Mr. Beans in the snow.

As Joey ran up the sidewalk to his house with Serena draped limply in his arms, he kicked the screen door, and called out desperately for his brother. He got onto the porch when the door banged open, and Wayne dashed out, taking Serena from him.

There are times in life when everything seems unreal. For Joey, this was one of those times. Just a moment ago he was outside playing in the snow with Serena; now he sat on the edge of Wayne's bed where she lay quietly with her eyes closed, like she was sleeping. He felt her slipping away from him, but there was nothing he could do.

He heard Wayne in the living room calling a rescue unit and Serena's mom. Then Wayne came into the room and sent him to the porch to wait for Serena's parents. Joey went reluctantly, and when he had gone, Wayne took Serena's hand and said out loud to himself, "I don't know what to do. Oh, come on, Serena. Don't die on me. Come on, little girl." But her eyes remained closed, her body still and peaceful.

Bowing his head, Wayne prayed. "God, what can I do?"

A heavenly light came over the room. Tess and Monica appeared at the end of the bed. With them was Andrew, an angel of death, and he said to Tess and Monica, "I'm glad you two are here."

"We just thought she'd appreciate a familiar face or two." Monica gazed down at Serena and knew it wouldn't be long now.

Wayne, oblivious to the light or their presence, continued to hold Serena's hand with his head bowed.

Tess stepped up to the other side of the bed and spoke to the little girl. "Serena..." When she heard her name, Serena opened her eyes, her face washed by the light. Tess continued, "This is our friend Andrew. He is here to take you to heaven very soon."

Andrew, the most handsome angel Serena had ever seen, knelt beside the bed and came down close to her. "It's going to be a beautiful trip, Serena. And you won't feel any more pain."

Serena smiled as Andrew went on, "That's right. There will be some difficult days until then, but your angels are here with you, and you will not be alone."

Tess bent over and patted Serena's arm. "Fear not, my little angel."

Wayne, still in prayer, didn't see or hear the angels, yet when Monica whispered in Wayne's ear that Serena's favorite song was "Silent Night," he started singing very softly, "Silent Night…" Tess joined in, although Wayne couldn't hear her. "…Holy Night…"

Out front on the porch Joey heard his brother singing as he sat there waiting for Serena's parents. He tried to find the words for a prayer. Then he voiced his fears. "Dear God, this is Joey. My heart wants to tell you something." He faltered, his voice cracking. "Please, don't let Serena go into the dark. Because if Serena goes to heaven, who's gonna love me? Please help. Love, Joey."

Monica appeared behind him and laid her hand gently on his shoulder as Joey rocked back and forth and Wayne finished the song. "Sleep in heavenly peace."

# CHAPTER
## Five

Joey knew his best friend was sick. But what he didn't know was that there was a possibility that she might not be there to open her presents on Christmas morning.

Maybe in his heart he knew, but none of the adults talked about it to him. And he refused to think about it.

Serena's mother led him into her little girl's room, where Serena lay in a hospital bed with an oxygen tank beside it. Close by was a tiny Christmas tree surrounded by brightly wrapped gifts.

"Look who's here, honey!" Serena's head turned slowly, and she smiled when she saw Joey. She looked so tiny in that big white bed with the steel railing.

Joey shifted from one foot to the other, overjoyed to see her. "Hi, Serena."

As Serena's mom went out the door, she warned him, "Don't forget, Joey. We have to be very still and gentle."

# A Christmas Miracle

"Okay," Joey whispered as he sat down next to Serena. "How come you have a new bed?"

Serena told him that he didn't have to whisper and that she had a new bed because she had to lie there for a time.

"Your mom says if we just wait a while you're going to get a new heart and then you'll be all better." Joey was optimistic, but Serena smiled with a new wisdom, with the understanding of a child who knew that death was near. "I don't think so, Joey. The other day I saw angels. Monica and Tess, the organ ladies, they're angels."

One of the wonderful things about Joey's childlike way was that he believed almost everything anyone told him. So when Serena said that the new strangers in town were really angels, he knew it must be true.

Joey said, "No! Real angels? They don't look like angels."

"They did when I saw them. They're beautiful, Joey." Serena's words inspired Joey and he told her that he wanted to see the angels, too.

Serena got very serious and asked Joey if he would do something for her. Of course, Joey eagerly agreed. She asked him to promise to take care of Mr. Beans. Joey's eyes got wide as he struggled to remember, but he couldn't, so he asked her, "Mr. Beans! Where is he?"

Serena looked sad. "I think I dropped him in the snow." Joey tried to think of the place he and Serena were making the angels outside. But he couldn't think of exactly where it was. "Joey, you have to take him to the Christmas pageant tonight. I promised Mr. Beans he could fly."

"But you're going to be the angel. You're going to take him up and fly like an angel."

She coughed and said, "No, Joey. I can't. But you can."

Joey looked scared. He wanted to please his friend, but this was impossible. "I can't go. It's at night. It's in the dark." His voice wavered as he pleaded, "I can't. You have to come with me."

"I can't take you through the dark anymore, Joey. You have to do it all by yourself."

He shook his head, muttering, "No, no, no."

But Serena encouraged him. "You can do it!" She smiled and repeated her line from the pageant: "Fear not!"

Fear not. Joey came face-to-face with his largest handicap and it wasn't physical. It was his own horror of the dark. His own dread of loved ones going into the twilight, never to return. Now here was his best friend in the world telling him that he'd have to face the darkness alone.


Joey charged down the snow-lined sidewalk, frantically searching for Serena's teddy bear, but he couldn't find the place where they had made the snow angels. A group of children passed by as he scanned the surface of the powdery snow.

He pleaded with them desperately. "Did you see an angel? Did you see Mr. Beans?"

The kids giggled nervously, not knowing what to think of this big kid acting so crazy. "Have you seen Mr. Beans?" The children continued down the sidewalk, laughing at

Joey. He tried his best to remember, knocking his knuckles on his head, but it was all a muddle. He gave up and slowly walked away, passing a garbage truck.

Trash collectors grabbed garbage bags from the curb where Mr. Beans lay hidden from Joey's sight. They tossed the trash and the teddy bear into the truck and sped away. Joey had stopped just short of finding Mr. Beans.


The church was ready for Christmas—fresh boughs of evergreens decorated the windowsills; the stage was set for the pageant that night. But Joey wasn't ready. He ran frantically from pew to pew, searching in vain for Serena's bear. "No, no, no."

When he got to the front pew he realized that he wasn't going to find Mr. Beans there. He may be lost forever and he wouldn't fly like Serena had promised. Sick at heart, Joey looked up at the manger scene: the stable Wayne had repaired earlier stood strongly at center stage, cardboard sheep and animals around it, the manger in the middle. His sorrow turned to anger. He leaped onto the stage and tore into the manger scene, wrecking everything he and everyone had worked so hard to create.

Afterwards, he sat down on the edge of the stage, out of breath, with his head in his hands. He stayed like that for a moment, then he looked up into the stage light and prayed, "Dear God, this is Joey again. I have a problem. I'm scared." He fought back tears as his voice quivered, "I can't find Mr. Beans and Serena is sick and I promised he'd fly and the Christmas pageant is at night, and...and..." He grew more and more afraid as he spoke.

Then there came a soft voice from the back of the church. "That's an awful lot to be afraid about all at once, Joey." Joey looked up to see Monica walking toward him.

"Are you an angel?" Joey fidgeted as he continued shyly, "Serena says you're an angel."

"Yes, I am."

"You don't look like an angel."

Monica smiled and sat down on the stage beside him. "Sometimes I do."

Joey confessed that he had made a mess. He looked back at the pile of cardboard and lumber that once was the manger scene, and rocked back and forth. "Wayne is going to kill me." Monica told him that she understood and she offered to talk to Wayne about it. Joey didn't say anything for a time, then he looked up at her and said, "Serena is going to heaven."

"Yes, she is."

Tears welled up in his eyes. "I'm going to miss her. I'm going to be all alone."

Monica put her hand on his shoulder. "No, you won't. You still have Wayne."

He worked up courage to say the painful words that came next.

"Wayne hates me." He said it simply and honestly, and that made it profound.

# CHAPTER
## *Six*

Joey sat on the sofa with his arms over his head, rocking restlessly. Monica was there, her hand soothingly on his shoulder, awaiting what she knew was coming. And it did.

They heard the door fly open, then slam. Wayne stormed into the room. A force of anger punctuated his words. "Joey!"

Joey's hands shook as he watched Wayne coming at him. "I'm sorry, I'm sorry!"

Monica wanted to reason with him. But reason was not present in Wayne's mind.

He yelled at Joey, pointing his finger at him, "What do you think you were doing? Do you know what you've done?"

Monica went to him, trying to calm him, "Wayne, please just listen…"

"Listen to her, she's an angel!"

A Christmas Miracle

"Shut up, Joey! It's a mess over there. You're lucky they're not going to arrest you!" Fury welled up in Wayne. All the times that he had had to make right what Joey had made wrong rose up before him. All the times that he had wanted to shout at Joey, but didn't. All the anger from those times overwhelmed Wayne and Joey was terrified to see his big brother like that.

Monica explained to Wayne that Joey was frightened, that he had reacted the only way he knew how. But Wayne wouldn't listen, saying that was no excuse.

"Yes, it is. He's your brother and he needs some understanding."

"Who do you think you are?"

Joey said again, "She's an angel!" Then he apologized to his brother.

But Wayne came back at him with, "You don't leave this house, do you hear me?" Joey wanted to know if he could go to the Christmas pageant. Wayne thundered back, "There IS NO PAGEANT!"

There was a look of panic on Joey's face. He couldn't hold back the pain any longer. He jumped up and ran up the stairs to his room. When he was gone, Wayne confronted Monica. "He thinks you're an angel."

"It's true."

"No, it's not, and I'd appreciate you staying away from him, okay?"

Monica tried to convince him that Joey needed hope, that without hope he had nothing. Joey also needed his older brother.

"All he does is need me. He can't even button his shirt without needing me."

"When I'm angry, I ask God for patience."

"What did God ever do for me? Give me a brother like that and then take my parents away so I got stuck with him? Ask God for patience? It was God who did this to me."

Monica remained calm and said, "That's not how God works."

Sarcastically, Wayne came back at her, "Really? Oh, I forgot. You oughta know. You're an angel. Look, this is none of your business."

"I think it is. Joey is my friend."

"Yeah, he's everybody's friend. Trouble is, he's nobody's responsibility— except mine."

"Responsibility is a privilege. You've been entrusted with a beautiful soul who loves you, who is loyal to you, who would never hurt you. He is your flesh and blood, he's the only family you have. And he needs more from you than room and board. He needs the love you want to give him, but won't. Why? Why won't you love Joey, Wayne? He thinks you hate him."

"What?" Had he heard her right?

"That boy who adores you believes his brother hates him."

Wayne was overcome. He turned away to compose himself, then looked back at her. "When I was a kid, I prayed for a little brother, and when I finally got one...well...

every morning I'd wake up expecting a miracle, hoping that I'd walk into the kitchen and he'd be sitting there at breakfast all fixed and fine. But the miracle never came, and I stopped believing in them. But something wouldn't let me give in, you know? Loving Joey means...I don't know."

"It means that you accept him as he is," said Monica.

Wayne dropped his head. This was true.

"Joey is not going to change. And maybe you can't handle that. But Joey has handled it beautifully." She stopped a moment, then continued, "But he needs you now, Wayne. He is losing Serena, and he knows that. And when he loses her, he'll lose the faith that has kept him going. He can't understand loss. But he can understand love."

"You're talking to the wrong guy. I've got no faith left."

"Just help Joey find his, and I promise you, you'll find yours. Make that pageant happen tomorrow night." She smiled at him.

Deacon Jamison and Edna carried pieces of broken card-board and wood down the front steps of the church as Wayne and Monica drove up in Wayne's truck. In the truck bed were tools and some lumber.

The deacon greeted them and Wayne apologized for all the trouble Joey caused.

The deacon said, "Well, don't worry about it, Wayne. The boy was hurting. Truth is, he did what most of us wanted to."

Wayne motioned to the broken pieces. "I was thinking maybe I could put a hand to those and fix 'em up for the pageant."

Edna tossed a broken cardboard sheep into the trash and said, "Well, that's sweet, but there's no pageant now, Wayne. Truth is, I think we were only doing it for Serena's sake in the first place."

Monica stepped forward. "Then isn't that a good enough reason to do it now? Maybe she can't be there, but promises were made. Shouldn't we keep them?"

But the organ was still broken. Broken—until suddenly there was a magnificent swell of organ music from inside the church. Full, melodic notes signaled that somehow the vintage organ was once again in magnificent working order. The music stopped, the window opened, and Tess leaned out. "Did you hear that? Did I fix that sucker or what?"

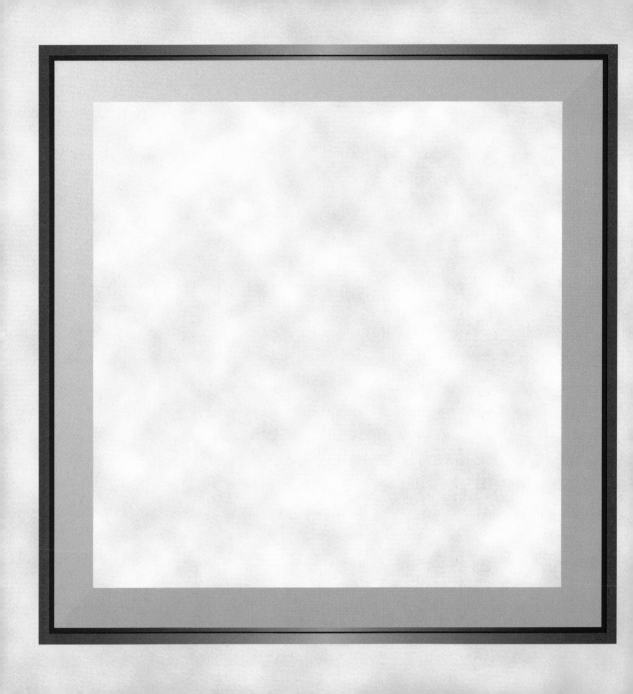

# CHAPTER
## *Seven*

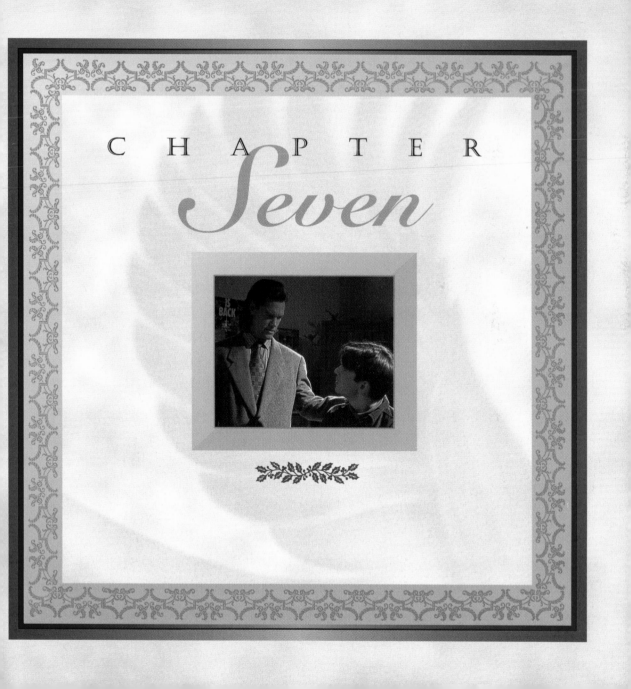

## A Christmas Miracle

Joey sat there in his room, alone with his thoughts about Serena. Was she really going to die like they all said, or would there be some kind of miracle? Why did she have to go? When his mother and father had died, he wanted to wake up and find out it was just a bad dream. It was like that with Serena, but he knew it wasn't a dream.

Behind him a figure loomed in the doorway. It was Wayne, dressed up for church. He apologized for the things he had said earlier, but Joey didn't want to talk to him. Wayne continued, "I know you hurt inside. I know you're worried about Serena."

Joey looked up at him. "She's going to heaven."

When Wayne told him that somebody might give her a new heart, Joey wasn't optimistic. Wayne went on about how it was important to have hope and how Serena was Joey's best friend, maybe even a better friend than he'd been. He sat

# A Christmas Miracle

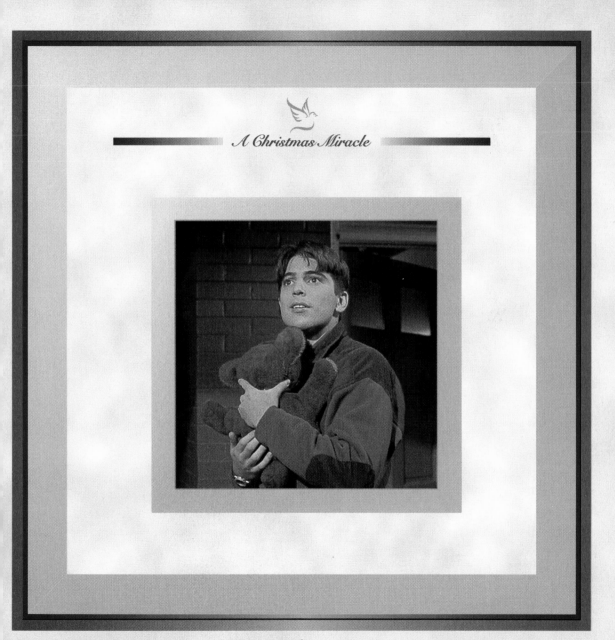

down on the bed beside Joey and said, "She's never tried to change you. And Joey, I'm not going to try to change you anymore. I love you, just the way you are." Joey knew that this was hard for Wayne to say. He couldn't remember him talking like this before and he wanted to believe him. He glanced over at Wayne.

"Where are you going with your suit on?"

"I'm going to the Christmas pageant."

Joey was surprised and reminded Wayne that he had broken everything. Wayne put his hand on his shoulder. "Well, I put it back together. It looks pretty awful, but it's standing!" Wayne motioned toward the window where Joey could see the night sky and invited him to go to the pageant, too. For a moment it looked like Joey might just brave the darkness, but he glanced nervously at the window and shook his head.

As Wayne came out the door onto the front porch he sighed deeply and looked up at the sky, like he was going to pray. But he didn't. He descended the steps and headed down the sidewalk.

At the door stood Monica. She watched Wayne disappear down the street and then she knocked on the door. After a moment, Joey peered through the window, saw it was Monica, and quickly opened the door a crack, careful not to step outside.

"Hello, Joey. Merry Christmas."

He opened the door a little wider and said, "Wayne is at church."

"I know. It's Christmas Eve. He's going to the pageant. Why don't you come?"

Joey shook his head. "I can't."

"I know, it's very dark out here. But you made a promise, didn't you?"

He stared at her in amazement. How did she know?

"Remember the promise you made to Serena?"

"But I lost him. I can't keep the promise because I lost Mr. Beans." Joey was anxious and agitated. Monica stepped aside to reveal Serena's green teddy bear sitting on top of the porch railing. Joey was stunned.

"Sometimes keeping a promise takes a lot of courage, Joey. Serena knows you have courage."

When he saw Mr. Beans, he smiled. Serena would be happy to see him again. Then he remembered the dark and the smile disappeared from his face.

"You've already been through the darkest place you can imagine. It's time to start looking for the stars." Monica went to the sidewalk, stopped, and looked back at him, smiling. Then she continued down the street. Joey stood at the door, looking at the dark sky, then at Mr. Beans.

He took a deep breath, mustered up his courage, rushed out, grabbed Mr. Beans, and was about to run back inside when he suddenly saw something: a star brighter than any other, supernaturally bright and beckoning. It had cast a glow over the street, creating an amazing path of light. Joey stared up at the star, clutching Serena's bear. Then he stepped off the porch, down the steps, out into the center of the street and followed the light. It flooded him with a peacefulness and a courage that he'd never known before. It lit his path directly to the church.

The pageant was in progress. Children dressed as Mary and Joseph with baby Jesus stood at the front of the stable and the choir was to the side. As Deacon Jamison read, the shepherds approached. "And lo, there were in the same country shepherds keeping watch over their flocks by night. And behold, an angel of the Lord stood by them, and the brightness of God showed 'round about them." Perfectly on cue, Harry plugged in a spotlight. The shepherds reacted melodramatically as the deacon continued reading. "And they were greatly afraid, and the angel said unto them: Fear—"

## A Christmas Miracle

From the back of the room came Joey's voice, bold and clear. "Fear not!" The congregation turned to see him as he made his way down the aisle reciting the lines, "I bring you good tidings of great joy that shall be to all people! Fear not!"

Wayne was moved to see his brother and he said, loud enough for everyone to hear, "I'm proud of you, Joey. You did good." Joey looked up at the angel harness where Serena should have been, then down at Wayne, who fought back tears.

The organ hit a harmonious chord and Edna banged away on the keyboard, leading the choir into a resounding Hallelujah Chorus. Nearby, Tess nodded a pleasant I-told-you-I'd-fix-it smile.

Joey sat down beside his brother, holding Mr. Beans. "Guess what, Wayne!"

Wayne smiled, "What?"

"You love me!"

"Yes, I do," Wayne said.

Joey beamed, "And, I love you." Wayne put his arm around Joey and hugged him.

Monica, who had been watching from the pew behind them, leaned forward and said, "I'm glad you came, Joey." As soon as he saw her he knew he might have a chance at fulfilling Serena's promise and asked her to help him.

While the choir sang and the play continued, Monica enlisted the assistance of Harry, who tried to convince her that what she wanted to do was dangerous—she was too heavy, it would never work. But Monica prevailed.

The wise men arrived at the stable with their gifts, as the choir sang, "The kingdom of this earth is become the kingdom of our Lord. And He shall reign forever and ev...er..."

In the audience, Joey was almost overwhelmed with excitement. He had walked by himself to the church in the dark. Well, not exactly dark, but it was night. And Wayne had said he loved him. Now he was waiting for Monica to help him keep his promise to Serena. It was the best Christmas he'd ever known.

"King of Kings! Forever and ever!" The choir was in high gear as Monica, strapped in the harness, rose from behind the stable with Serena's teddy bear. She glided up over the stage and toward the audience. For a moment she floated there and Joey was thrilled. But the rope that supported Monica twisted and frayed, and got thinner with each reach of the sopranos. Everyone there saw it—the desperate look on Harry's face, then the rope snapped. And what happened next was not grounded in earthly logic or reason. All who witnessed it would be changed forever.

A bright, white light flooded the sanctuary. The sound of the choir became louder, richer, accompanied by trumpets and heavenly music. "King of Kings, and Lo-ord of Lords! And He shall reign, and He shall reign…"

Instead of falling, with great pageantry and power, Monica ascended over the choir, suspended, unattached to any pulley or harness. She was dressed in splendid angel raiment and glory literally shone 'round about her, and a

heavenly wind caught her hair and her clothing, creating
the impression that she had wings.

The stunned congregation was too overcome to do or
say anything. But the choir somehow was compelled to
continue, as the cardboard prop animals transformed into
live beasts right before their eyes—sheep, goats, even a
camel!

Monica soared there for what seemed like an eternity,
smiling benevolently. Then she dropped Mr. Beans, and
as Joey and the audience watched, the bear changed into a
dove and flew away. Wayne and Joey stood up. One by one,
the people of the congregation rose to their feet. Joey
knew this would happen all along. Now Wayne would real-
ize that what Monica had said was true: she really was an
angel.

Voices from the back of the church joined in with the
choir up front. Everyone looked up toward the choir loft

and saw a choir of real angels, flanked by two herald angels trumpeting, singing in the radiant light.

Brilliant illumination filled the entire room, almost blinding. Some in the congregation even covered their eyes. On the stage, a divine light shone from the manger. The nativity scene became more real—the clothes, the gifts, the animals. The shepherds and wise men fell to their knees, not melodramatically but realistically, emotionally, honestly, in reverence.

Only Joey and a few others saw what came next. In a corner, near the front of the stage, stood Tess with Serena and Andrew. Serena looked well, dressed in her Christmas best and waved goodbye to Joey. He waved back and beamed, knowing he had kept Serena's promise, and she knew it, too.

The evening air was cold and crisp. The star still shone brightly on the little church as the choir could be heard inside singing, "Hallelujah! Hallelujah! Hallelujah! Hallelujah!" Tess, Monica, and Andrew led Serena down the sidewalk, into the street beneath the star, and disappeared as an entire flock of white doves rose to fill the night sky.

# CHAPTER
## *Eight*

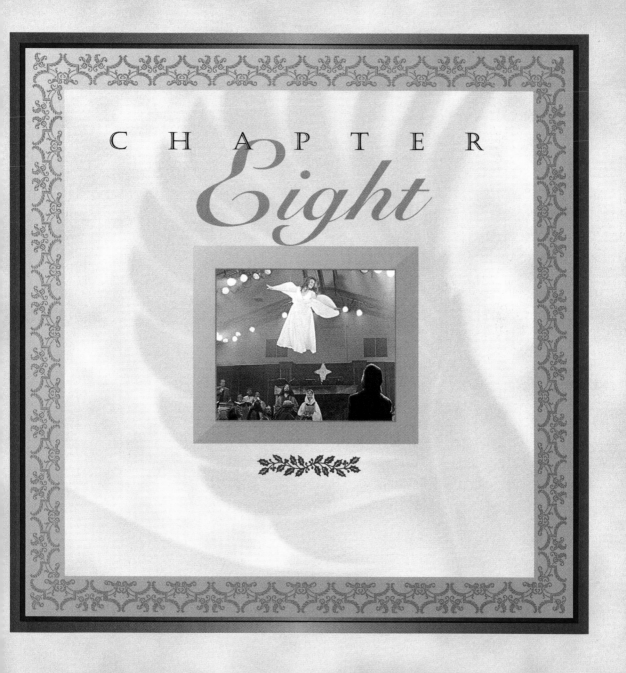

## A Christmas Miracle

Wayne awoke from a fitful sleep. He had been dreaming about the night before when the angel flew, and how Serena's bear turned into a dove, and how astonishing it all was. Joey burst into the room, excited about it being Christmas, and pleaded with Wayne to let him open his presents. When Wayne said he could, Joey tore off toward the living room.

Wayne looked at himself in the dresser mirror and said, "What did you have to eat last night to make you dream about flying angels, buddy?"

Joey returned to remind his brother that he wanted to go back to church to see the angels. Wayne was unclear about it all. It was just a dream, wasn't it? Or could something like that really happen? He crossed to the window. A dove that had been perched outside on the sill flew away as Wayne gazed out over the new snow.

*A Christmas Miracle*

# A Christmas Miracle

Tess and Monica appeared behind him, but he was unaware of their presence as he spoke, "I'm no good at praying, you know. Real praying, that is. I suppose after what happened last night I'm supposed to believe in You. Well, that's not gonna be easy. 'Cause if You're really out there, then I'm in trouble. So, I appreciate the angels and all, but I'd just as soon pass, thank you."

Monica spoke to Tess, although Wayne couldn't hear her. "He knows the truth. He saw it. Why is he afraid to believe?"

"The first day one believes can be the most beautiful. And the most difficult."

Monica didn't see how it could be difficult. From the living room Joey called for his brother. Wayne pulled on his robe and slippers.

Tess tried to help Monica understand. "Well, a miracle is a fragile thing. If you don't take care of it, you can let all the truth get twisted right out of it. And that's when it gets dangerous."

"How can miracles be dangerous?"

"Anything from God can be dangerous in the wrong hands." Wayne sat on the edge of the bed, deep in thought, oblivious to being the subject of the angels' conversation. Tess continued, "Now Wayne—he's a man who has walked in darkness for a long, long time. A miracle like the one last night has shone a bright light, but it's shining smack on all the things that Wayne doesn't want to see."

"So he can't get on with his new life until he finishes his old one?"

Tess nodded and replied, "He's at a crossroads. You got to get him out of the intersection before he gets run over." And then she spoke slowly and with deliberation. " 'Cause somebody's speeding in his direction and he's about to get hit head-on."

The miracle that happened in church on Christmas Eve was the subject of almost every conversation the next day.

## A Christmas Miracle

Were you there? Did you see it? What was it like? Was it true that a child's toy had transformed into a dove, or was it a cherub, as some had said?

The Star Diner downtown became miracle headquarters, with groups of townspeople milling around, drinking coffee and telling what they knew about the angel flying. So when the handsome stranger arrived, no one much noticed. He kicked the snow off his cowboy boots at the door and asked a waiter about getting some breakfast, only to find out that they weren't serving breakfast yet on account of what happened the night before.

Charles, who had just gotten into town, could tell that something important had occurred by the way everyone was talking so loudly. He pieced together the story about the angel flying from the things they said and noticed that the ones who were the center of attention were the ones who said they had been there when it happened. Some people thought the angel would return. Some believed it was a once-in-a-lifetime event.

Then Charles asked the waiter, "Could you give me some directions to this church? Miracles are kinda my business." That set in motion a whole scheme that was inevitable. If it hadn't been Charles, it would have been some other con man.

Only five minutes passed before Charles was on the diner phone, talking to a regional television station. "That's right, a Christmas miracle. Yes, it's true, I saw it myself and so did everybody else. It was kinda scary, kinda awesome, all at once. You'd better get a news crew down there right away, and if you don't I'm calling Channel Ten next." He paused a moment, then smiled. "All right, you're welcome." He hung up, looking awfully smug, and walked away.

He passed Tess and Monica as he headed out the door. They were not pleased. Monica asked, "Tess, why does God make men like that?"

Tess reassured her, saying, "He doesn't. They make them-selves like that. The sad truth, baby, is that where there's an opportunity, there's an opportunist. And nothing brings 'em out like a good old-fashioned miracle."

Word of the miracle spread far outside the town's city limits and visitors from all over crowded into the church to see for themselves the holy place where the miracle had happened. Joey figured it was probably because everybody wanted to be closer to God, one way or another. He stood on the church steps, handing out programs to people as they entered. "Merry Christmas! Merry Christmas!"

At the curb, Charles got out of his car and popped open the car trunk. He looked like he'd just had a shower and he wore a clean suit. Inside the trunk was a suitcase, and inside the suitcase was an array of religious paraphernalia—golden crosses, a communion cup, rosary beads. He pulled out a Catholic clerical collar and started to put it on, but turned to check the sign out front which read: Washington Park Community Church. He tossed the collar back in and grabbed a cross on a chain.

When Charles asked Joey for a program, Joey saw the cross hanging around Charles's neck and said, "You came to see the angels, didn't you? That's why I came. I saw the angels last night, too."

"Did anybody else see the angels?"

"Oh, everybody. My brother, and Edna, and Pastor Mike, and everybody. The angels took my friend Serena up to heaven. And one angel, she turned into light and flew high up into the sky. And then the white bird flew away but he dropped a feather and I got it. See?"

Joey showed him a white feather. Physical evidence of a miracle. Charles was intrigued, but acted like he was unimpressed, took a program, and went inside. Moments later Joey realized that his feather was gone.

Inside was chaos. Congregation members argued about who had seen what the night before. Strangers wandered around, inspecting every nook and cranny. The cardboard nativity scene from the pageant attracted souvenir hunters and Edna, who played the organ distractedly, had to shoo people away to keep them from ripping up pieces of the scenery to take home.

She played the organ louder, then finally called out, "Everybody's supposed to sit down when they hear the organ!" Very few complied.

Charles parted the crowd and came to the front, finding a seat in the first pew.

Pastor Mike went to the microphone and implored everyone to sit down. Joey stood at the back door because there were no more seats. The pastor paused for a moment, searching for the right words. He seemed at a loss on how to proceed. Sighing deeply, he began, "Last night something happened here that some are calling a miracle."

## A Christmas Miracle

A parishioner shouted out, "It was a miracle!" Another asked, "But what does it mean?" A third stood and said, "It means we're doomed! Judgment is coming!" Then a man in the third row insisted that he had seen the little girl who had died last night, right there in the church, and he saw the angels take her away.

Pastor Mike tried to regain control of his flock and explained that Serena's passing may have been part of the miracle, but that this was something they must take one step at a time. Slowly, reverently. A member of the congregation asked why they must proceed slowly.

He tried to explain, "We have been given a marvelous gift, a mystery has occurred in our midst, a holy visitation. We must not greet it with panic or superstition. We must cherish it, keep it in our hearts until we have learned what God intends for us to do with it."

But the parishioners began to murmur and were growing restless. This wasn't lost on Charles, who was assessing his chances of taking advantage of the situation. One man

pointed out that some people had slept there the previous
night, and that Harvey Osborn thought it was the beginning
of the end of the world. And that Clara Otis said her rheuma-
tism was getting better, and Amy Tassler said hers was getting
worse. What in the world was going on?

Pastor Mike didn't know what to say. He had never had a
miracle like this happen in his church before, and he was
unprepared. The congregation sensed his uncertainty and
they began talking among themselves, drowning their pastor out. Edna, sensing the beginning of trouble, took mat-
ters into her own hands and started pounding out "Angels
We Have Heard On High" on the organ. This only added to
the confusion.

Suddenly a TV news crew, headed by reporter Gina West,
rushed up the aisle toward the stage. They were all business
and in a hurry. The congregation fell silent. Edna stopped
playing.

Gina West stuck the news microphone in Pastor Mike's
face and snapped, "Gina West, Channel Eight. We're here

to check out the miracle. This is the place with the flying angel, isn't it?" This set off a wave of whispers that swept through the pews. And when Gina West asked who had seen the miracle, Charles stood up tall and, with great authority, said, "I saw the angel!"

A hush came over the room as everyone strained to see who it was. The news crew was on Charles within ten seconds of his admission of being a first-hand witness to the miracle.

Charles played to the camera. "Folks, I'm a stranger here. But last night I saw a light in the heavens, a light brighter than anything I'd ever seen." Charles spotted Joey at the back of the church.

"You saw it too, didn't you, son? The light in the sky?" Joey nodded excitedly and said the angel had shown it to him.

Tess and Monica, unseen by the congregation, appeared on the stage beside Edna at the organ. They gave each other an oh-brother look as Charles continued with his deceptive tale.

"That's right. The angel. The most beautiful sight I've ever seen. An angel all in flowing white. I was an itinerant preacher who'd lost his faith, but then I saw the light of God last night and it led me here, to this sacred place. I stood in the back of this church, tears of joy on my face, as the light from the angel cleansed my soul." His electrifying "Elmer Gantry" act took over the church. The news crew loved it.

Pastor Mike tried to interrupt, but Charles ignored him and went on, "And the most miraculous sight of all was the light turning into the most pure of God's creations on earth—a dove. And for those of you who may be doubters, I have proof." He reached into his jacket and dramatically produced Joey's white feather, waving it in the air before the entranced congregation.

"Hey! That's my feather!" Joey said loudly.

But Charles answered back, "That's right, son. It's yours." Then pointing to other parishioners, "And yours. And yours. It belongs to us all. A gift from the heavenly creature itself. As the dove flew past me, this feather…this beautiful reminder of God's presence floated down to me like manna from heaven." Everyone was swept up in his excitement and crowded around Charles. Everyone, that is, except Monica and Tess.

Monica was incredulous. "Tess, why are they believing all this?"

Having seen it all before, Tess replied, "Because he's telling them what they want to hear. They are eager to embrace the miracle, and eagerness is what a con man loves best of all."

# CHAPTER Nine

eople had taken care of Joey all his life As soon as it was apparent that he would have special needs, his mother turned most of her attention to him. This left the rest of the family to look after themselves. When his parents were gone, Wayne stepped in, and because Wayne was always busy with his work, Joey experienced a little independence, a little self-sufficiency. But he wondered if he would ever be on his own, or if he would live with Wayne the rest of his life.

Joey thought about things like this when he was alone, like today while he picked up used programs from the empty sanctuary. As he moved up the aisle, he saw Monica sitting in the deserted pews. He greeted her excitedly and yelled out to anybody who might be left in the church that the angel was back.

"Ah, no, Joey. I'm just here for you today," Monica explained.

A Christmas Miracle

As soon as he saw her, he had questions. Did the other angel take Serena up to heaven? Monica acknowledged that this was true, that Tess had helped.

Joey asked quietly, "Serena's not coming back, huh?"

"No, she's not." Joey nodded and fought back the tears. Monica continued, "But I want you to know that Serena is very happy where she is today."

Monica touched his shoulder gently. "It's okay to cry, Joey. I know you miss her."

"Serena was my friend and she took care of me."

"I know. But Joey, maybe it's time that you started taking care of someone."

This was a hard thing for Joey to get right in his mind. He couldn't even take care of himself, how could he take care of somebody else?

At that moment, there was a rustling noise that came from the nativity scene. Joey turned toward the stage and the distinctive sound of a baby's cry came from the stable.

### A Christmas Miracle

Joey went to the manger and looked down. Slowly, a smile came over his face. There, lying on the straw, was a baby. Joey knelt down in awe. He looked back for Monica, but she was not there. He lifted the infant out of the manger very carefully, wondering if this was baby Jesus. If he was, he was too late; everybody had gone home.

Joey had never held a baby before, but he remembered seeing other people doing it, and he had picked up a puppy once. He brought the baby up close to him, awkwardly at first until the baby stopped crying. Joey sat on the edge of the stage and rocked it in his arms, humming a hymn from the pageant.

The church fellowship hall was filled with media—television news crews, newspaper reporters with their photographers, and tabloid editors. The churchgoers who had witnessed the miracle drank coffee and gave interviews.

But it was Charles who was the center of attention, surrounded by the press and parishioners, including Edna. Across the room, Pastor Mike watched with growing concern as Charles performed for the cameras. Charles said to Edna, "I knew this was a special place the moment I walked in. People want to believe, and this is about to become a place of great belief. It happens every time I hold a revival. Get ready for the onslaught."

Edna asked Charles what he meant by "onslaught."

"People don't experience miracles every day, if ever. They want to see where they happened. Once in San Antonio a mob almost leveled a church; they were splintering pews with axes to get relics. Oh, well, that probably won't happen here. Nice meeting you all." He started to leave, but Deacon Jamison stopped him and asked him to stay a while longer. Then Deacon Jamison huddled with the other deacons and Pastor Mike to talk about the possibility of Charles staying on a few days to deliver a sermon or two. From the look of it, Pastor Mike wasn't getting his point across.

## A Christmas Miracle

Joey stopped at the doorway and peeked in. He didn't have the baby with him, having left it in the manger. He tried to get Edna's attention, but she was busy with Charles, talking about whether an "onslaught" would mean more money for the church, because it could certainly use a refurbishing.

"You have a building fund, don't you?" Charles asked. When Edna told him that they didn't, he saw his opportunity. "Ah, yes, this requires some finessing. In Tallahassee I came across the same situation. We took the charity fund and temporarily made it the building fund. And we invested in the church and in the community by adding on and building up. Attendance increased so fast that in one month we replaced the charity fund and doubled it!" That sounded good to Edna.

Joey came into the fellowship hall and asked Edna to come with him. He had something to show her, and it wasn't a puppy. But Edna was too busy, according to Charles, who dismissed Joey like some messenger boy with bad news.

So, Joey left, disheartened. Who was the right person to tell about the baby? Where were the angels when he needed them?

The meeting of deacons broke up and Pastor Mike, clearly displeased with the outcome, headed for the door. Deacon Jamison returned to Charles and Edna and said, "Pastor Charles, I think I speak for everyone when I say we'd appreciate all the help we can get. We'd like you to hold one of your revivals here."

With false humility, Charles replied, "I am not worthy. But thank you, I'd be honored." Then Edna invited Charles to join her family for Christmas dinner, and he gladly accepted.

The church was empty, except for Joey sitting in a pew with the baby. He was waiting for Wayne to pick him up and he wasn't quite sure how he was going to tell Wayne. He had considered not telling his brother and smuggling the baby into his room like he had done with a young bird that had fallen out of its nest. But if Wayne could hear a baby bird peeping, then he would surely hear a real baby crying. So he decided to just tell him outright, and he rehearsed aloud. "We have a new baby brother." Then Joey looked back at the baby with a questioning look on his face. "Or is it a sister?"

The sound of the door closing made Joey look around to see Wayne coming down the aisle toward him.

"Hi, Wayne."

"Who are you talking to?" Wayne stopped at the pew and looked down.

Joey glanced up at Wayne and smiled. "Your Christmas present." He lifted the baby up proudly. The bewildered look on Wayne's face said it all.


Having no idea what to do with a baby, Wayne decided to take it to the hospital. There a young nurse, Jackie, told him the news. It was a little boy, and there was something else.

"A crack baby?" Wayne was surprised.

Jackie explained, "Lots of drugs in the baby's system. It's tragic."

Not far away, Joey stood gazing through the window of the newborn nursery. His baby looked so helpless, lying there all alone in that plastic bassinet. What would become of him? He felt a burden in his heart for the baby. Monica was right, it was time for him to take care of someone else—but would Wayne let him?

A nurse, really Tess in a hospital uniform, looked over Joey's shoulder at the babies and asked, "Which one is yours, honey?"

Joey delightedly pointed to his baby. When Tess admitted that it was her favorite, he recognized her. He blurted out, "Hi! You're the angel. Are you a nurse now, too?"

Tess let him know she was there to watch his baby and he was relieved that the baby had an angel of its own. After

talking for a few minutes with Tess about babies, Joey realized that there was a lot he didn't know about taking care of
a life so fragile. But Tess encouraged him, explaining about
the baby's mother taking drugs, how she abandoned him,
and how the baby needed him now.

When Joey asked what he could do, Tess replied, "Well,
for starters, these babies haven't been held or loved enough
and we don't have enough nurses to rock them. Being
rocked makes them feel better."

"Can I rock my baby?" It wasn't Tess, but Wayne that
answered, with an emphatic, "No." Joey looked around to
see Wayne beside him.

Wayne thought it was a bad idea for Joey to take any more
time with the baby. He knew how easily attached to things
Joey got and this could become a very difficult situation.
When Joey insisted on rocking the baby, Wayne became
more determined to break this off before things got out of
hand. If it hadn't been for Tess interrupting and calling
Nurse Jackie over, Joey wouldn't have gotten to rock his

baby. Nurse Jackie assured Wayne, "Babies in this condition need special attention. They've been so deprived that any love Joey could give would really help."

Later, in the nursery, Joey in a hospital gown, sat in a rocker with his baby. Tess was nearby, cradling another infant in her arms, humming a traditional lullaby: "What Child Is This?" to the tune of "Greensleeves."

After that Wayne started bringing Joey to the hospital every day to help take care of the baby. He learned to give him a bottle, bathe him, and change his diapers, but his favorite thing to do was rock him. Tess and Jackie were there to teach him whatever he needed to know. And when Wayne saw what a positive effect all of this had on Joey, he lightened up a little.

One day at the hospital, when Joey went to put on a hospital gown, he left Wayne with Jackie and the baby. It was apparent to Joey that Wayne liked Jackie. After all, she was very nice, and very pretty, maybe the most beautiful nurse

Joey had ever seen, and it would be good for Wayne to have a girlfriend, although he never told him so.

When Wayne asked Jackie how the little guy was doing, Jackie smiled and said, "Much better. At this rate, he'll be needing a home soon. Hint, hint."

"Oh, no, not me. I've got my hands full with Joey."

"Maybe you could do it if you had some help."

Wayne played along, "And what makes you think that's a good idea? Nurse's instinct again?"

"You're learning," she smiled back.

After Wayne had gone, Joey asked Jackie what was going to happen to his baby. She told him the truth, that as soon as the baby was well, they would have to find him a home.

He looked at her anxiously and said, "I have a home for him."

"Joey, it takes a lot to be a parent."

"Do you have to be smart? 'Cause I know I'm not smart."

## A Christmas Miracle

She asked him if he knew what babies needed—food, clothes, and eventually school. Could he provide all that for a baby? Joey realized that he couldn't and that the hospital would find a home for his baby. A home that would separate him from the baby he had grown to love. He felt sad and was frustrated that he wasn't smart and he desperately wanted things to be different.

After realizing that his future with the baby was unsure, Joey spent as much time as he could at the hospital. It didn't even seem like Wayne minded bringing him there, maybe because he liked seeing Jackie.

During one of the visits, Wayne stood at the nursery window watching Joey rock the baby. He was touched by the love that his little brother shared and the sensitivity with which Joey held the baby's tiny hand.

Wayne was aware of someone beside him and looked around to see Edna there with flowers. She had come to visit a sick parishioner and was surprised to hear about Joey finding a baby in the manger.

"Oh, my. Miracles just keep happening," Edna said. "You must meet the new pastor. Well, it's not official yet, but I think it will be. Do you know in one week he's almost doubled the charity fund? Yes, Pastor Charles is something else."

When Wayne heard that name—Pastor Charles—something clicked. Something from a long time ago he had tried to forget.

"Pastor Charles, huh? You know, Edna, maybe we will stop in."

"Sunday morning, bright and early. Don't be late if you want to get a seat."

Then Edna waved at Joey in the nursery and headed down the hall. Wayne was left alone, haunted by thoughts from the past.

# CHAPTER
## *Ten*

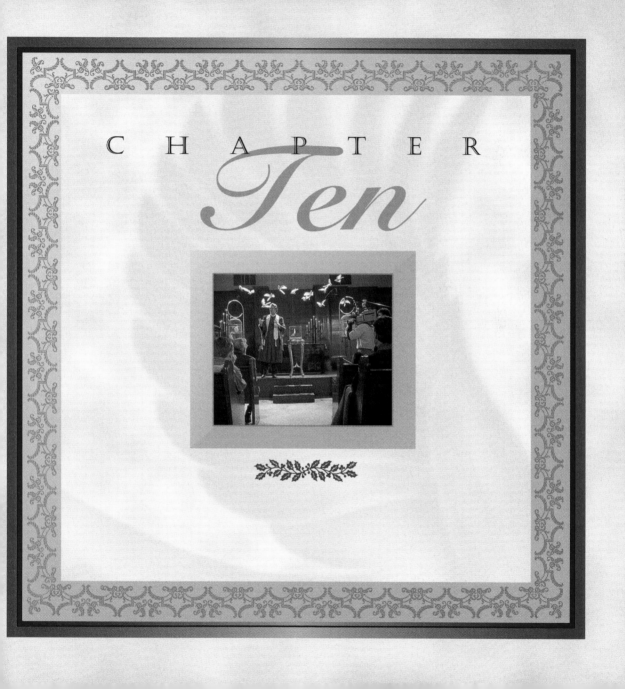

## A Christmas Miracle

There's one thing you can't buy with money, and that's a miracle. But when Wayne and Joey approached the church that afternoon, throngs of visitors were buying anything they could relating to the Christmas Eve visitation. There were T-shirts with "Feather From Heaven" emblazoned on the front, baseball caps, white plastic doves, and feather pins. Huge speakers stood on the lawn, bringing Charles' words outside. "An angel of the Lord visited us right here!"

Charles had his back to the congregation, his hands raised in exaltation, as Wayne and Joey pushed their way through the crowd inside. The church had been transformed—a flock of synthetic white doves dangled by monofilament line over the altar; cages of live doves flanked the stage; shiny new candelabrum were loaded with lit can-

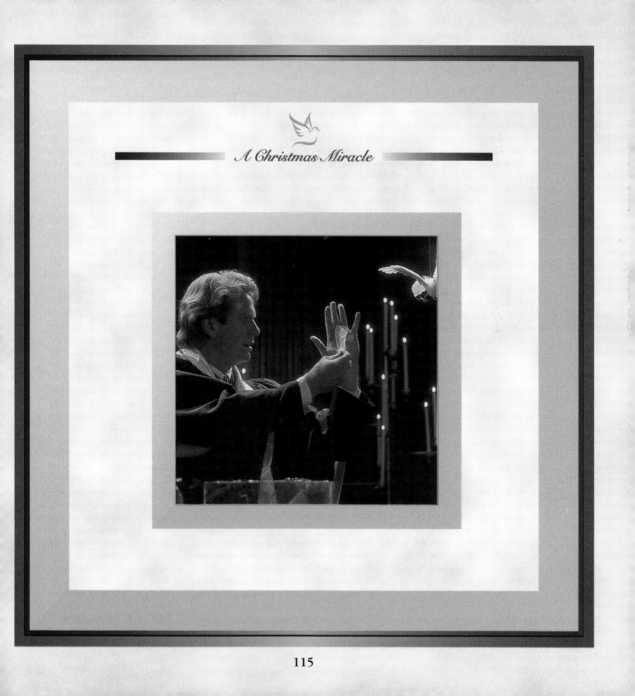

*A Christmas Miracle*

dles. It was a beatific sight to Joey, especially Pastor Charles, in his brilliant blue robe surrounded by all that splendor.

The service was being televised live, and a video camera operator circled Charles as he worked his way to a glass case gilded with gold. Inside was Joey's white feather, the feather from heaven. Joey noticed that most of the parishioners wore gold feather lapel pins.

Charles turned to the congregation and relayed his newest version of the story. "And a feather dropped from that dove. And I did not pick up that feather—the hand of God picked up that feather and handed it to me!"

Knowing it wasn't so, Joey said loudly, "That's my feather."

Wayne's worst fears were realized when he saw Charles. He pushed Joey toward the door, but Joey didn't want to go. When Pastor Charles saw Wayne there was a look of recognition on his face, and of understanding, as if a missing puzzle piece just fit. Wayne met Charles' insightful gaze with one of disgust, then pressed Joey toward the door.

"What are we leaving for, Wayne?"

"We don't belong in there, Joey."

At the bottom of the church steps, Monica greeted them. Joey was delighted to see her and said, "There you are! Where'd you go? It's the angel, Wayne."

Wayne was shocked. After all, the last time Wayne had seen her was Christmas Eve, when she was hovering over the church amidst what had seemed like the very presence of God. But now he suspected that she was connected with Charles, and Charles was a con man. Maybe they had set the whole scam up from the beginning. He didn't know how, but now it was starting to make sense. Wayne glared at her and told Joey, "She's no angel."

"You know I am, Wayne."

"I don't know what you are. Maybe a magician, probably a con artist just like…" He stopped himself, aware of his little brother listening to every word. "Joey, meet me in the truck."

Joey left them alone and Wayne continued, "I don't know what happened in there on Christmas Eve. Some kind of mass hysteria or special effect show probably..."

"Don't talk yourself out of the miracle, Wayne. The presence of God was in the church that night."

"Have you been in there today? I didn't know God was in the T-shirt business now."

Monica glanced over at the T-shirt booths lining the sidewalk. "He's not."

As she walked with him toward the street he said, "Well, somebody is. If that's what miracles do, then I'm not interested in God."

"What you're not interested in is this "religion" that Charles has just created to take advantage of a lot of vulnerable people right now. It's happened for centuries—people trying to explain the unexplainable, and giving their souls over to someone who claims to speak for God."

He came back at her bitterly, "If that's got your boss upset, what are you doing out here? That man inside there is a con artist."

"He is also your brother." The truth resounded as if spoken with loud cymbals. Wayne looked at her, amazed that she knew and admitted that Charles was his brother. He'd put a lot of time and space between them and there was no way she could have known that—unless she really was an angel.

She confirmed again that what he said was true.

"Then there really is a God?" He looked away, as if he were assessing this new information. "And He knows what I used to do?"

"Yes, He does."

"Well, what if I don't want to believe in Him?"

"That's certainly your choice, but it's not going to make Him go away. God is real, Wayne. And the miracle was real. And God wants the people of this church to know the difference between the truth you all saw and the myth that's taking its place. "

"I can't fight my brother."

"You're the only one who can."

He wished that Charles had never come to his town, that he had never heard about him from Edna, and that he had never brought Joey there that day.

When he looked over at the truck where Joey was supposed to be, he saw that the truck was empty. When he looked back to ask Monica if she had seen where Joey had gone, Monica wasn't there either.

Joey crept back in to see Pastor Charles deliver his sermon. He wanted to hear more about his feather, more about the angel. And, like everyone else, he was mesmerized by Charles' charismatic style and his golden tongue.

"I had a message from the Lord last night. A powerful, fearful visitation. From the angel sent by God to this very place not one week ago. She was not the vision of glory and Christmas love this time, however, my brothers and sisters. She had a terrible aspect upon her face and a fearful message: God is not pleased!"

Neither were Tess and Monica, who were watching from the choir loft with frustration and disbelief at the outlandish statements Charles was making.

A murmur ran through the congregation as Charles continued, "God told me He does not want this holy relic, this consecrated feather, to be relegated to a glass case. He has other plans. This feather is not just a feather, but the very Finger of God Himself!"

About then, Wayne came in the back looking for Joey. He was just in time to hear a murmur of shock and questioning from the pews. Charles had them. Suddenly he pulled out a hammer and smashed the glass case, shattering it. The crowd gasped. But the performance was just getting started. Then Charles took a broken piece of glass and pulled it across the palm of his hand dramatically. There were cries of horror and disbelief from the sanctuary as blood appeared on Charles' hand. Then he picked up the feather, and ran it over the cut and, miraculously, the blood disappeared and the wound "healed." The crowd was near frenzy.

Monica shook her head as she and Tess beheld the exhibition from the loft, but Joey was both thrilled and fascinated by what he had seen.

"We are being led, dear brothers and sisters, to a time of healing. This feather is God's Christmas gift, and all who believe shall be healed by it. So, friends, there will be a healing service tonight."

Wayne made his way through the people, unaware of what had just taken place.

Charles continued his rhetoric as Wayne found Joey and dragged him out the door. "Let this sacred token of God's power heal the infirmities of every believer. The more you believe, the deeper your healing."

"I believe," Joey whispered.

## A Christmas Miracle

Later that day, Wayne's truck pulled into the parking lot of a local cheap motel. Inside one of the bungalows, Charles practiced his disappearing blood trick when a knock came at the door.

It was Wayne, and he didn't look like he was there for a happy family reunion. But Charles greeted him matter-of-factly, as if there had never been trouble between them, almost glad to see him.

"Well, it's my little brother! Come in, I've been expecting you." Charles held up his hand with the fake blood and said, "I'd shake your hand, but I've got to wait for the disappearing ink to disappear first. Wanna drink?"

Wayne was strictly business and got right to the point. "What are you doing here? " he asked, staring at Charles with a cold, unsympathetic look.

Charles wiped the ink from his hand, poured himself a drink, and said, "Hey, look, I was just passing through. Didn't have any idea you lived here. At least, not until I heard about the angel. Man, what a scam. Hope you don't mind, I just couldn't help jumping on your train, little brother."

"This isn't my scam and it isn't my train." Wayne was incensed at the suggestion.

"How many you got on the payroll? Some special effects guy definitely, maybe two, and obviously some chick to be the angel. But I don't get it. Why haven't you cashed out? What's your angle?"

There was no angle, Wayne told him. There was no con. There really was an angel, the miracle really happened. And besides, he was out of that life now.

Charles stared at him for a moment, then smiled and laughed, "You know, all these years, you were the ringer and I did the talking. It shoulda been the other way around—I almost believe you."

"Look, I don't expect you to understand this, but I'm not gonna let you take what happened to those people and turn it into something cheap."

Charles sat down on the bed with his drink and put his feet up. "Turn what into something cheap? There is no God! You know that and I know that. Now don't get me wrong. I wish there was a God. Man, I could use one right now. But all I've got is me. And that's what I believe in."

"You can believe anything you want, Charlie, as long as you believe this too: If you don't pack up and get outta town right now, tonight, no healing service, I'm gonna blow the whistle on you. I don't want to, but if I have to, I'll let the local police know about the twenty-thousand-dollar building fund that disappeared from that church in Wisconsin."

Charles stood up and faced off with his brother. "That whistle blows both ways, you know. They connect me, I connect you." He said it almost tauntingly, like he was daring Wayne to tell.

Wayne's eyes narrowed and he snapped, "I didn't steal that money. You did."

"That's the way you remember it." The words were not completely out of Charles' mouth when Wayne grabbed him by the shirt and shoved him up against the wall. All the anger leftover from those past years with Charles boiled up in Wayne and threatened to explode.

But Charles was almost amused, and said, "You were great at this, you know. A natural. Remember that night in Chillicothe, Missouri? You got up from the back, crying 'Heal me, mister! I got a turr'bl disease!' You huffed and puffed all the way up the aisle, I coulda sworn you were gonna die on me right there."

Wayne relaxed his grip as Charles continued, "And the more I prayed, the sicker you got. I coulda kicked you. And then, all of a sudden, you slapped that look of absolute, beatific, heavenly glory onto that baby face of yours! Lord, what a haul we raked in that night!"

As Charles reminisced about the "good old days," an odd look came over his face and he asked, "Whatever happened to the kid?"

"Your brother's name is Joey. He lives with me now."

Charles shook his head with pity and said that he thought for sure that that pathetic little creature would have been in some kind of home by now.

Wayne stood there staring at Charles, fighting back the rush of rage. How could a man look so innocent, yet be so deceitful? Then he said in a caustic tone, "You just finish your business here and get out of town."

Wayne left before he did something that he would regret.


When he was outside, he took a deep breath of the crisp, clean air and walked to his truck. And there was Monica.

"You can't just walk away from him, Wayne."

"He's got me, Monica. If I try to stop him, he'll take me down with him. And I'm not saying I don't deserve it. But if I get put away, what happens to Joey?"

Monica answered, "God doesn't want you to lose Joey. But He doesn't want your brother to rob these people of their money or their trust or their faith. And you have to have faith that if you've been chosen to do something, God has a good reason for it."

"And I've got a good reason."

"Think what you're doing, Wayne. God loves you, Wayne. He came right into that church on Christmas Eve to tell you so. He took away your disbelief. If you walk away from Him now, you do so knowing exactly Who you're turning your back on. And if a man walks away from God, where else is there to go?"

Wayne said he didn't know, but he was afraid he was going to find out.

# CHAPTER

## *Eleven*

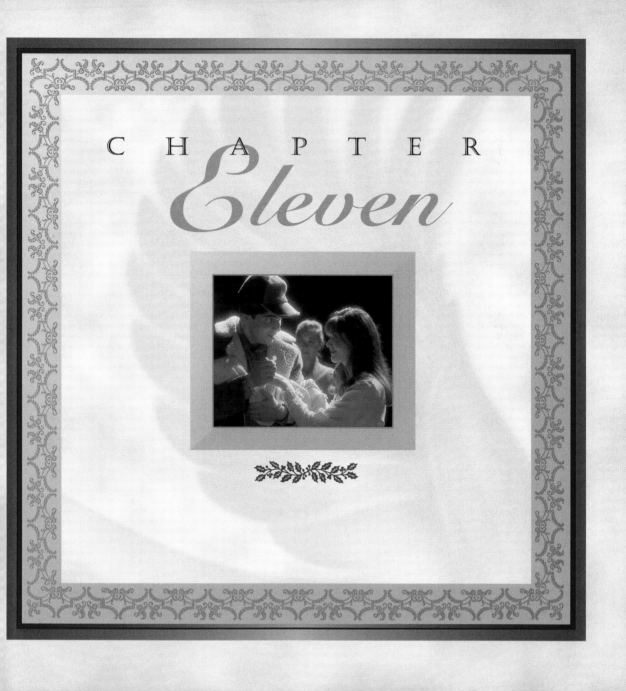

Streets glistened with melting snow that night as Wayne drove Joey in the truck. Joey was getting used to going out at night, a little at a time. He daydreamed about the healing service that he was determined not to miss and wondered how it was going to be when he got smart. Would Wayne look up to him? Would people at the church treat him differently? And most importantly, would he be able to teach his baby important things, like arithmetic and spelling?

Hostility from Wayne's confrontation with Charles remained strongly etched upon his face when Joey said, "I'm happy, Wayne. Because tonight I'm gonna be made smart and then we can have the baby. We'll have to give him a name."

"Joey..."

"I don't know, Wayne. If we named him Joey and my name is Joey, how would we know who you were talking to?"

A Christmas Miracle

Wayne told him that they weren't going to get the baby
and nobody was going to make him smart. But Joey
explained that the man in the church was going to heal him,
that he did miracles from God.

"No, he doesn't," Wayne said.

"No, I saw it, you didn't. The man's hand was bleeding
and he touched it with my feather and it stopped."

That was a trick, Wayne said. But Joey didn't want to
believe it. If that was a trick and he didn't really stop the
bleeding, then the man couldn't heal him. And that was
something that he didn't want to think about.

"A long time ago, the man in the church and I used to
trick people together."

A funny look came over Joey's face and he asked Wayne if
the man in the church was Wayne's friend. Wayne waited a
long moment before he answered the question. Then he
told him.

"No. He's our brother."

Joey was silent, like he had to play those words back again in his head before he was sure of what Wayne had just said. Then, quietly he said, "He is?"

He'd been away a long time, Wayne explained. But Joey couldn't understand that if he was their brother, why had he taken Joey's feather, because people aren't supposed to steal. Even Joey knew that.

"Yeah, Charlie hasn't changed much. If it's not nailed down, it'll be in his pocket within the hour. That's why I left him and came back."

"To take care of me?"

When Wayne confirmed that it was true, Joey asked why Charlie didn't take care of him. Wayne didn't have a good answer for this.

To Joey it was like a fairy tale or something. A story that Wayne read to him out of a book. Suddenly he had two brothers. It was all very confusing, especially since Wayne didn't seem to like Charlie.

They stopped at a traffic light and Joey looked over at Wayne. "If you could, would you touch me with the feather and make me smarter?"

"You know I would, Joey."

"Charlie's my brother too, so he'll touch me with the feather and make me smarter."

"No, Joey. You're missing the point." Wayne tried to hide his animosity toward Charles, but Joey could see it clearly and it made him afraid. "Charlie is a liar and a cheat and you stay away from him."

Joey pleaded with him, "But it's my only chance to be smart."

"You don't have a chance to be smart!" Wayne spit it out like sour milk and immediately regretted it. There was a silence between them, a horrible quiet that trapped them in that moment.

Joey searched for words and then said, "Yes, I do."

He jumped out of the truck and ran, fleeing into the dreaded darkness with Wayne's hurtful words ringing in his ears.

Wayne shouted after him, "Joey! Joey! I'm sorry! I'm…" But Joey was gone.

Christmas decorations still graced the door to the maternity ward as Joey hurried up to look through the glass in the door. When he saw Jackie leave her station at the counter, he slipped into the nursery.

The babies were asleep, but even with their eyes closed, Joey could tell which baby was his. He scooped him up and held him close, then escaped out the door with his baby, unnoticed by the nurses.

A little while later, Wayne charged through the door and went right to the nursery window, where he discovered the empty bassinet. He alerted Jackie and they went into the nursery and saw Joey's baby was missing.

Joey's heart beat fast as he rushed down the sidewalk through the puddles of melted snow, cradling the infant in his arms. He was afraid someone would find them and take the baby away. He didn't know where to go or what to do. He had to think of a plan. But he wasn't much good with plans. A moment of fear came over him, then suddenly he remembered.

"I'm not sure which way the church is. But the angel told me if you find the star, it will light the way. So all we have to do is…"

Joey looked up to see a bright white star and a smile came to his face. He cuddled the baby to him and took off down the dark street toward the star.

## A Christmas Miracle

It was the healing service that Charles had announced. Once again, the sanctuary was full. A banner above the altar read: "Believe and Be Healed." As Edna led a hymn from the organ, ushers passed baskets to collect the offering. And a generous one it was, heaps of bills flowing over the top.

Charles, wearing the billowing, purple robe of a minister, bounded up to the pulpit and the crowd broke into spontaneous applause. He was fully in his element now and jumped right into the service by asking, "Are you ready to be healed?"

A thunderous "Yes!" resounded from the pews.

"Have you brought your faith with you tonight?" When another booming "Yes!" came from the sanctuary, Pastor Charles asked, "Is there a doubter in the room? Because we can't do anything if there is."

By this time he was almost prowling the stage. The crowd was getting worked up as he exclaimed, "Are you believers in the power of the feather? Believers in the power of the angel?"

"Yes!" was the answer. And Edna clapped her hands and shouted out, "Hallelujah!"

Charles called for the offering trays to be brought forward. Four ushers delivered four baskets brimming with cash to the altar, then sat down in the sanctuary.

Then Charles dramatically turned his back to the audience, as they had seen him do before, and he stood before the baskets to offer a prayer. Everyone closed their eyes and bowed their heads as Charles prayed.

"Oh, God, bless these poor offerings of the heart, these simple tokens of the wealth that lies in every grateful heart that has been touched by this life-giving miracle."

About that time, Wayne came in the back with Jackie, searching for Joey. They stopped in the crowd beside Pastor Mike, who looked like he was having trouble keeping quiet.

Charles continued, "Grant that every believer will receive healing tonight according to his faith. Amen."

Pastor Mike shook his head in disagreement. "No, no, no. It's not only according to faith, but by the mercy of God Almighty."

Whispering, Wayne asked Pastor Mike if he'd seen Joey. He hadn't, but had Wayne been listening to this? "He's taking away everything that's holy and blinding them with smoke. What have I done?"

Many parishioners raised their hands as Charles turned to face them, producing the feather, raising it above his head. "No matter what the ailment, you can be healed if you believe in the power of the feather."

He walked down the aisle passing the feather over eager parishioners, quickly touching the hands of each. Some people swooned. Others appeared to be in rapture.

Suddenly Joey stood up from a pew and started toward Charles, carrying the baby. Many raised their hands, but only one voice was heard above the others: "Me! Me! Charlie? I'm next."

Wayne started to go after him, but Jackie stopped him.

Pastor Charles came down the aisle. "Who said that? Come on up here! Some people call me Pastor, or Brother, but you can always call me Charlie!"

Then he saw Joey with the tiny baby and understood what confronted him. This was exactly what Charlie needed to avoid, a handicapped boy who would appear exactly the same after the healing. It wasn't good for business.

Joey headed for the front proudly and expectantly. "Hey, Charlie, it's me!"

Charlie still didn't recognize him and was caught off guard. "Sorry, kid, I don't do diapers!" There was some nervous laughter from the audience.

Joey stopped in the middle of the aisle and said innocently, "I wanna be smart like you, Charlie. And this baby, he needs to get all the drugs outta him so I can take him home and take care of him. But you gotta make me smart first."

There was absolute silence in the hall. Charles cleared his throat and glanced over at Edna, who waited with fading anticipation. He was going to heal Joey, right?

"Aren't you gonna put the feather on me?" Joey started toward Charles, but a loud voice came from the back of the church. "No, he's not." It was Wayne.

Joey looked back as Wayne and Jackie approached. Wayne laid his hand on Joey's shoulder.

"But he's my brother." Joey didn't understand. If Charlie had used his feather to heal all those people just now, why couldn't he heal him, especially since they were brothers?

At the front, Charles stared at Joey, as if seeing him for the first time. "Joey?"

Happy that he finally recognized him, Joey said something that didn't come out exactly as he had intended. "Hi, Charlie! You stole my feather."

A wave of whispers rolled through the audience.

Struggling to recover from the nasty revelation, Charles countered that it didn't matter where he got it, it was still the feather from the dove.

"How would you know? You weren't even there!" It was Wayne this time who spoke, sending another shock through the pews.

Charles waved the feather in the air and warned Wayne to be careful. Deacon Jamison came up the aisle and stopped beside Wayne, asking if Pastor Charles was really his brother.

Wayne nodded. "I'm afraid he is, Deacon. But he's no Pastor." And, with a sigh he said, "He's a thief."

A murmur of protest rose from the congregation, until Wayne stalked up the aisle to the altar and grabbed Charles's robe, revealing hidden pockets filled with cash from the offering baskets. Wayne held fists full of money up for everyone to see. A collective gasp was heard and Charles stood there in humiliation.

"He's a hustler, folks. I'm sorry. I shoulda told you sooner. It's just that…well, I used to be just as bad as him. And ever since this miracle, I've just been waiting for God to come and punish me. I guess this is just the beginning of it."

Charles called to his friend Edna for support, but she snapped, "Don't you 'Edna' me. Now you take that robe off before I take it off you. Man of the cloth. I don't think so!"

He removed the robe. People were starting to stand up and walk out when one parishioner said, "So, there was no miracle!"

Wayne corrected her, "No, there was a miracle. I won't pretend it hasn't complicated things something awful, but there was an angel. I saw her. And I know that God didn't send her just so we could all be at each other's throats."

One of the parishioners asked what it had all been for. The answer came in the form of a voice they'd heard before. "It was a Christmas present."

Everyone turned around to see Monica walking down the aisle, glowing radiantly, and every bit the angel she was the last time she appeared to the congregation.

There were gasps and whispers: "It's the angel!" "That's her." "Look! She's back!"

A magnificent light filled the church. Monica's radiance illuminated Joey, the baby, Wayne, and Charles as she approached them.

"The miracle was a little glimpse into heaven, a gift from God to the faithful people of this church whose roof may be leaky and whose organ may be ancient, but whose door was always open to the sick, the poor, the lost..." Then she smiled at Joey and put her hand lovingly on his shoulder. "...And the simple. But you took the gift and let someone ruin it. You worshipped a feather and an angel instead of a King, you sought out fame instead of the needy, you embraced the loud arrogance of pride and became deaf to the tiny voice of a baby in the manger. The cries of this lost child were answered only by one soul."

The churchgoers began to look ashamed as she continued, "The rest of you turned your back on the truest love of
all. You exchanged the miracle for a lie."

One woman with tears in her eyes appealed to Monica,
"Please, will you tell God that we're sorry?"

Monica said that they could tell Him themselves. That
was what God was trying to reveal to them on Christmas
Eve: He was listening.

The truth of the angel's words pierced the lies that had
filled the room and no one moved, no one spoke. Finally,
the silence was broken by a call from Joey. "Then, God, if
You're listening, God, can I have my feather back?" It was
an honest plea, a heartfelt one.

Monica went to Charles, who was utterly shaken. She
held out her hand and he slowly delivered the feather to
her. She, in turn, gave it to Joey and told him that the
feather wouldn't make him smarter. He admitted that
Wayne had said that, too.

"God doesn't care how smart you are, Joey. He cares about what's in your heart. And the love in your heart gave a forgotten little baby the will to keep living. God has a plan for this baby and the family waiting for it. And you have a family, too."

Joey looked over at Wayne and Charles, then carefully handed the baby to Monica. He took the feather back to Charles and said, "So, Charlie, guess what?"

Charles was overcome with emotion. Tears flowed down his face as his little brother took off his hat respectfully when he approached, looking somehow smarter than he ever had before. "What?" asked Charles.

Joey held out his precious feather. "You can have the feather back, 'cause I don't need it anymore."

Charles took the feather from Joey. "Neither do I."

"You've been faking the miracles for a long time, Charlie. What's it like to finally see a real one?" Monica waited for an answer.

Charles tried to speak, but his words got caught in his throat. He looked to Wayne, tears in his eyes. Wayne saw his pain and it looked a lot like his own. He said softly, "Yeah, I know. Me too."

Finally, Charles composed himself and confessed, "All these years…I didn't think about it. I didn't know that I was making up lies about Somebody real." He stopped a moment, realizing how powerful this revelation was. "God help me."

Monica smiled reassuringly and said, "He will. Just ask."

Charles shook his head, repentant for all the terrible things he had done in the name of God. Then he dropped the feather as he lifted his hands and surrendered his heart completely to the Lord. As the feather floated gently toward the ground it was miraculously transformed into a white dove.

Everyone watched the dove as it flew away. When they looked back, Monica was gone and a murmur went through the congregation.

## A Christmas Miracle

Charles, having just experienced his first real miracle, held his hands to his face and wept. Wayne put an arm on his big brother's shoulder and said, "Come on, Charlie, let's go home."

The two brothers embraced like they never had before, opening their arms to include Joey.

Edna, with good timing, hit the organ keys with gusto and the choir began to sing "Angels We Have Heard On High." The congregation joined in as Charlie, Wayne, and Joey turned to walk down the aisle. Jackie, still holding the baby, joined them, and they all walked through the crowd together.

Outside a new snow fell as the angels came out into the street away from the church. Joyful voices filled the night as Edna led the hymn inside.

Tess looked awfully pleased with their work there and said, "Now that's what I call a miracle."

"How come people only notice them at Christmas?" Monica asked.

"Well, we're working on that, angel girl. We're working on that."

*A Christmas Miracle*